THE
Convenient
Vegetarian

Quick-and-Easy Meatless Cooking

Virginia Messina
and Kate Schumann

Macmillan • USA

MACMILLAN GENERAL REFERENCE USA
A Pearson Education Macmillan Company
1633 Broadway
New York, NY 10019-6785

Macmillan Publishing books may be purchased for busi-
ness or sales promotional use. For information please
write: Special Markets Department, Macmillan Publishing
USA, 1633 Broadway, New York, NY 10019-6785.

Book Design: George McKeon

Cataloging-in-Publication Data is available from the
Library of Congress

ISBN 0-02-862334-7

Manufactured in the United States of America

10 9 8 7 6 5 4 3 2 1

Contents

Acknowledgments

As always, this book would not have been possible without the help of wonderful friends, family, and inspirational cooks.

Neal Barnard, president of the Physicians Committee for Responsible Medicine, generously shared recipes from that organization's "Vegetarian Quick Fix Contest." We're especially grateful for his help. We also want to thank the wonderful cooks who submitted winning recipes to that contest: Evelyn Wootton, Danny, Seo, Kimberly Erickson, Linda Means, David Beapre, Julie Humiston, Dorleen Tong, and Doris Krauch. Their recipes have become among our personal favorites, and we are very grateful to have the chance to include them in this book. We racked our brains for what to call our section on how to use leftovers and are most thankful to friend Kathy Constantine for sharing the term *planover* with us.

As always, we offer heartfelt thanks to our agent Patti Breitman for her enthusiasm and warmth. Thanks to our editor, Jim Willhite, for his guidance, skill, and cheerful manner. We're indebted to all of those at Macmillan, for their encouragement and belief in this project.

Finally, and as always, we are grateful to our husbands, Ned Schumann and Mark Messina, taste-testers extraordinaire.

Quick-and-Easy Meal Preparation: Strategies for Success

Getting dinner on the table with as little effort and time as possible is a high priority for most of us. And of course, we want our meals to be healthful and delicious. *The Convenient Vegetarian* answers these challenges in a new way that we think you'll enjoy and find useful. It's much more than a collection of recipes. It's a compilation of strategies for fast meal planning and preparation as well as a manual on how to organize your kitchen and your cooking time, how to shop, and how to stock your kitchen. Be sure to read "Getting Organized": You'll find ideas that will really make your time in the kitchen easier.

If you are new to a vegetarian diet or have questions about creating a healthful diet, then our nutrition primer and information on meal planning will help you feel confident about the basics of a well-balanced vegetarian diet. We'll also show you how to rethink menus so that simple and fast add up to great nutrition. In addition, we'll share some ideas for menus that come together in minutes without any recipes or special preparation instructions.

This book revolves around four strategies for fast meals:

- **Convenience cookery:** Your grocery store shelves are packed with convenience products that fit right into vegetarian menus.

We'll introduce you to some of our favorites and share recipes that take advantage of these wonderful products.

- **Fast and fresh:** Although convenience foods are great, they aren't always necessary to pull together a fast meal. Simple dishes that take advantage of a few fresh ingredients can offer spectacular flavor. We'll share some ideas for speedy meals with fresh taste.

- **Quick mixes:** These mixes are an updated twist on an old cooking standby. Cooks of the 1950s and 1960s used Master Mix, a basic baking mix, to save steps in creating a variety of baked products, including muffins and cookies. We've taken the idea a few steps further by creating mixes for all kinds of dishes, such as rice pilaf, chili, and potato soup, all perfect for vegetarian meals. These are homemade convenience foods, prepared in a few minutes at a fraction of the price but with many times the flavor of the store-bought variety.

- **Planovers:** We have a new way of thinking about leftovers. Plan to set aside a portion of a favorite recipe, and we'll show you how to use it as the basis for a completely different dish the following night. It's easy. Leftovers from Southwest Black Beans (page 150) on Monday night are resurrected as Black Bean and Corn Chili (page 152) on Tuesday. Spicy Lentil Soup (page 153) becomes Lentils with Dried Fruit over rice or Spicy Lentil-Rice Cakes (page 155). We'll share ideas to get you started and some tips to help you create your own Planovers.

Whether you love to cook or are a novice vegetarian cook, taking advantage of these strategies will make healthful eating easier than you ever imagined. Although the heart of this book is the recipes, we hope that you'll take some time to read the other sections as well. You will learn that some of the best ideas for making delicious, fast meals do not involve recipes at all. Be sure to read about meals that don't require recipes (pages 40–41) and take a look at our list of favorite vegetarian convenience items (pages 29–32) and tips for creating gourmet leftovers (pages 148–149) and your own delicious wraps (pages 146–147).

1.

Getting Organized

ORGANIZING YOUR KITCHEN

Fast recipes and meal ideas make life a little easier; but let's face it, there is more to meals than cooking. How you shop, organize your kitchen, and store your food will all affect how fast and easily you put dinner on the table. Efficiency in the kitchen truly means taking a big-picture approach to all of these tasks.

The "perfectly organized" kitchen is really a matter of personal preference and individual needs. In a nutshell, it means being able to find everything you need as quickly as possible and having the things you use most often close at hand. It also means storing the things you use near wherever you use them. For example, it makes better sense to keep the pot holders near the stove than near the sink. There are exceptions to this, of course. For example, even if you reach for dried spices and herbs while you are cooking at the stove, it makes better sense to store them away from sources of heat to maximize their retention of aroma and flavor.

Storing food and cooking implements in the most efficient and useful fashion possible will speed up the entire cooking process. The easiest recipe in the world can stretch into a long chore if you spend fifteen minutes looking for the oregano. But, of course, your personal cooking style and your kitchen design will dictate what works best for you. Here are a few ideas about what works in our kitchens.

1

- Store things where you can see them. We like food stored in glass jars on open shelves or in cabinets with glass doors. Obviously, it just plain makes it easier to find things. You'll also have a better idea of what you have on hand to make grocery shopping easier. Save large jars from pasta sauce to store dried beans and grains, and use smaller jars (like mustard jars, for example) to store bulk powdered broth or seasoning mixes. You can also find jars at yard sales and flea markets. We love square ones, because they make the most efficient use of space and they look pretty.

- Create storage space with shelving or free-standing bookcases. Hanging baskets are nice for onions and fruit or even to store boxes of tea.

- Buying in bulk saves money and time, but finding storage space can be a challenge. Think creatively and beyond the kitchen. Why not store cases of canned goods under a bed or in a hall closet? A shelved corner in the basement can become a perfect pantry.

- Make small items like herbs and spices more accessible by using a lazy Susan. If you use a lot of herbs, try a double-tiered lazy Susan to create even more space.

- Create a step in your cupboards by putting a 2×4 at the back of the shelves. Smaller canned goods or jars stored in the back will get boosted up a few inches so that you can see them more easily.

- Buy according to your needs. Many vegetarian items like dried beans and grains have a long storage life, but they don't keep forever. You don't want ten pounds of pinto beans taking up space if you cook with pintos twice a year. On the other hand, if you go through a certain item in record time, do stock up. It saves shopping time and money.

- Store ingredients near one another if you use them together often. For example, if you bake oatmeal cookies every week, it makes sense to have the flour, sugar, oats, and baking powder all stored on one shelf, preferably somewhere near the preparation area if that's possible.

- Keep an area of the counter available for food preparation. You may not have miles of countertop, but setting aside one small square that is free of appliances and mail and that will accommodate a cutting board and bowl can make a big difference.

Cooking in a Tiny Kitchen—A Sailboat's Galley

For four years my kitchen was about a quarter of the size of a very small half-bathroom! We lived on a thirty-six-foot sailboat; and my galley, as it is called, lacked all the modern conveniences—no running water (we used a foot pump instead), a stove with two small burners, an oven the size of a tiny bread box, limited pantry space, and no refrigeration. Only when we lived near a town or a marina were we able to get ice for our cooler. Yet we consistently enjoyed healthful vegetarian meals. The key was organization and storing things where I could get to them or remember where I had put them.

Clear plastic jars with tight-fitting lids were essential. Into those went herb mixtures, rice and lentil pilaf, and other mixes that I put together ahead of time. We stored onions in the mesh bags that citrus fruit often comes in, and we put grapefruits in old nylon stockings with a knot between each one so we could see if they were starting to go. Even now, with my good-sized kitchen and plenty of storage space, I still use some of those organizing techniques. When it comes to remembering where things are, out of sight, out of mind seems, unfortunately, to be my motto; thus I always try to arrange items so that I can see things quickly and get to them easily.

A typical easy-to-prepare dinner meal on our boat included lentil and rice pilaf with reconstituted freeze-dried French green beans (when we were not near a town where we could get fresh produce) with toasted pine nuts, Irish soda bread, and sliced oranges for a light dessert.

ORGANIZING FOR SHOPPING

Conventional wisdom has it that the proper way to plan menus and shop is to carefully plan out a week's worth of menus, run around the kitchen to see what you need for those meals, and then head for the store. If this doesn't work for you, don't worry. We have a better idea that takes less time, saves money, and allows for a slightly more free-spirited approach to menu planning.

Shop from a master pantry list, not for specific meals. The idea is to keep your kitchen well stocked with all of the foods and ingredients with which you cook. Simply keep track of what you have run out of over the past few weeks and shop to replenish those items. By keeping your kitchen well stocked, you don't need a weekly menu. You can make whatever you like, whenever you like, because—with the exception of certain items of fresh produce perhaps—you always have everything on hand that you need. This approach will also save you money, because you can stock up on things when they go on sale or hold off a few weeks on a particular item to see if it does go on sale. To keep better track, mount a blackboard on the wall and jot down items when you run out of them. It makes it easy to put together a shopping list. Once your kitchen is well stocked, you may find that a big weekly shopping trip becomes a thing of the past. We dash into the store a couple of times a week for twenty minutes to get fresh fruits and vegetables, but once a month is enough for big grocery store excursions.

You may find that buying some items in bulk makes this strategy even easier, and it is definitely an important way to save money on grocery bills. Explore food co-ops and membership warehouse stores for opportunities to save on bulk purchases. Discount grocery stores are also good options. If you have room for a freezer (even one sized for an apartment), you will be able to more effectively stock up on sale items or the foods you use a lot, like frozen juices, bread from the bakery thrift store, and frozen vegetables. Be creative about maximizing your storage space, because the more you can store, the less often you need to shop, the more money you can save, and the less likely you will run out of something important.

ORGANIZING YOUR COOKING TIME

If you and your spouse, significant other, or kids enjoy cooking togeth-er, why not set aside a few hours on the weekend to cook for the week ahead? It's fun and efficient. Because our recipes are fast and most will keep for several days in the refrigerator, you can prepare a week's worth of recipes in just a couple of hours. Or make two of the base recipes in the "Planover" chapter, and build on those throughout the week. If you don't want to cook whole meals ahead of time, you can do a little bit of preparation to speed up cooking later in the week. For example, spin the lettuce for salads, tear it into bite-sized pieces, and store it wrapped in a paper towel in a tightly sealed plastic bag. Or cut up big bags of vegetables and shred a bunch of carrots for salads and side dishes for the week ahead. You might also decide to use a few hours over the week-end to stock your pantry and refrigerator shelves. Why not make two or three of our salad dressings, label them, and tuck them into a shelf on the refrigerator door? They will keep for weeks. Or toss together a variety of our quick mixes so that you have a selection of your own homemade convenience foods at hand.

Zen of Cooking

Even though this book is about the quick-and-easy preparation of vegetarian food, there is always time to enjoy the moment; it will cer-tainly make cooking more pleasurable.

Just as you take time to select the best produce or to pick the greenest bunch of broccoli; the perfect head of cauliflower; or the tomato that's ripe, plump and juicy, take time when you are slicing or preparing these vegetables. Admire the brilliant red of the red bell pepper and be amazed by its myriad seeds, rub fresh herbs between your fingers to release their aroma, and be tantalized by the fra-grance of garlic and ginger sautéing together. When you are rinsing grains, beans, or greens for salads, be aware of their textures as well as their colors. Such mindfulness won't be time-consuming, but it will add to your cooking enjoyment.

Organizing for Entertaining

The older I get, the more casual my dinners for company become. Gone are the days of elaborate, many-course meals with everything made from scratch, including the French bread! Gone too are the artery-choking appetizers, sauces, and desserts. I was aghast when I found in the back of an old cookbook a copy of a menu for one of my dinner parties from the early Julia Child French-cooking days; it started with a Roquefort mousse stiffened with whipped cream, moved on to a sauce thickened with egg yolks over peeled asparagus, a roast of lamb stuffed with chicken livers and wrapped in rich pastry crust, and ended with yet another mousse—this time a Kahlúa mousse with more whipped cream! It's a wonder we lived to have another rich meal.

Nowadays I often serve Black Bean Soup with Fresh Lime and Cilantro (page 158) or Mushroom Risotto with Sun-Dried Tomatoes and Artichokes (page 58) as a main course. On the side, I'll serve a tossed green salad and wonderful crusty French bread with seasoned olive oil; for dessert, it's fruit, such as poached pears or delicious store-bought sorbet. Instead of a rich appetizer, we start with fresh veggies to dip in a sauce such as Red Pepper Tofu Spread (page 112). The soup, pears, and dip can all be made the day before. And the risotto can be prepared up until the final cooking stage, which then takes only an additional seven minutes in a pressure cooker.

Another popular casual entrée is homemade pizza. Use prepared focaccia as your crust and spread it with tasty bottled tomato sauce. Then top with sautéed vegetables (such as zucchini, onions, and mushroom), sliced artichoke hearts, and sun-dried tomatoes. Garnish with chopped black olives.

For a more formal meal, try the prizewinning Portobello Mushrooms Stuffed with Spinach and Herbal Pâté (page 93). Serve a salad of baby greens with our Balsamic Vinaigrette with Mustard (page 89)—it is a gourmet delight.

Truth be told, aside from the basics of cookery—pots and pans and a few good utensils—there is nothing that is essential to every kitchen. You'll have to look at your cooking style and decide what you absolutely need to have. After all, one cook's microwave oven is another cook's waste of space.

But we have a few favorite items that we couldn't live without. We believe that these items make life easier in the kitchen, and we'll share our ideas for must haves here. It was easy to come up with this list. We just thought about the items that we grab almost every day to make dinner.

Big **colander.** Buy a colander that is wide and deep and that will stay firmly planted on its feet when you drain even big, heavy pots of pasta or potatoes.

Big **cutting board.** Choose one that gives you lots of room to maneuver when chopping large vegetables like a head of cabbage.

Food processor. Most come with a chopping blade as well as a slicing blade and shredder. The better models, which have bigger motors, also have a plastic blade for mixing cookie or bread dough. Food processors do so much, they really are a huge help in the kitchen, for chopping vegetables and nuts, shredding cabbage for coleslaw, slicing vegetables, and blending ingredients together.

Garlic roller. Place a clove of garlic inside this little rubber cylinder, give it few quick firm rolls with the palm of your hand and the skin is completely removed from the garlic. It's a great timesaver for those who often cook with fresh garlic. (Kids love them, too; this is a fun way to involve children in food preparation.)

Good knives. You need not pay top dollar to have good knives. Just look for those with a good, sharp blade and a handle that feels comfortable in your hand. Then be sure to keep them well sharpened.

Immersion blender. This simple tool can be plugged in and then used to blend ingredients right in the pot. We use it to make cream soups and sauces—much easier than cooking the ingredients and then

What's for Dinner

Lest you think that we are the world's most organized, plan-ahead cooks, I should admit that I often have absolutely no idea what I'm having for dinner until I'm well into its preparation. When I find myself in the middle of the kitchen in a complete daze, wondering what I feel like cooking or eating, I will usually chop up an onion, mince a few cloves of garlic, and set them to sautéing in a bit of olive oil. Then I start rooting through my cupboards and cookbooks to see what comes next. But chances are quite good that whatever it is, it will start out with sautéed onions and garlic. It might end up being old-fashioned corn chowder, southern-style ranch beans, lemony roasted potatoes, or risotto. Whatever I decide, by the time I know what I'm having for dinner, I'm halfway there!

pouring them into a blender or food processor and then back into the pot. The immersion blender saves cooking steps and clean-up time.

Mouli grater. If you need a food processor only to grate vegetables, a Mouli hand grater is an inexpensive alternative. It has four different discs to give you options for grating size; the legs on the base fold up for easy storage, and they are quick and easy to clean.

Pressure cooker. We are both big pressure cooker fans. Nothing can beat them for cooking up great flavor, fast. Grains and beans that usually take a long time to cook are ready in minutes in a pressure cooker. This pot also provides an easy way to make dishes like risotto and polenta, which require lots of stirring and attention when made by more traditional methods. The new pressure cookers are safe and easy to use.

Salad spinner. We eat lots of salads, and this is a good way to make sure greens are well cleaned but nice and crisp.

Toaster oven. If you cook for just two or three people, you'll find a toaster oven adequate for most occasions. We rarely turn on the big oven, because we can toast, bake, and broil in the toaster oven, which saves on energy. If you are in the market for one, be sure to get a model that will take a decent-sized casserole dish or pan (9 × 13 inches). You'll find some toaster ovens even have two racks.

Vegetable steamer. We can't imagine cooking without this handy appliance. Almost any vegetable can be cooked in a steamer basket, and steaming is a method that helps retain nutrients.

2

A Quick Guide to Vegetarian Nutrition

Learning how to cook vegetarian style is one thing, but what about planning meals that will meet your nutritional needs? If there are special needs in the family—young children, a mom-to-be—these concerns are even greater. Fortunately, it is easy to plan healthful vegetarian diets for anyone, at any stage of life.

First, let's quickly clear up some misconceptions about vegetarian diets. You may have heard that vegetarians need to be careful to get enough of all the nutrients in their diet. The truth is, everyone needs to be careful to plan adequate diets, no matter what kind of eating pattern he or she follows. Every diet pattern has its strengths and weaknesses. But study after study shows that vegetarian diets have unique strengths and are truly beneficial in preventing and treating a host of diseases. Given that, it is well worth any effort to plan well-balanced vegetarian diets.

Protein is often a worry for new vegetarians, but it is an unnecessary one. Yes, vegetarians do eat less protein than meat-eaters, but they still eat plenty. There is no evidence that a high-protein diet (higher than what the average vegetarian eats) has any health advantages. But there is evidence that keeping your protein intake to a moderate level does have its advantages, because too much protein can be harmful to bone health and may raise the risk of kidney disease in some people.

You will get all the protein you need as long as you eat a variety of plant foods and you eat enough food to maintain your ideal weight.

In Western cultures, meals are planned with high-protein foods at the center of the plate. That is, for most Americans, meat, fish, or poultry is the main dish or entrée, and everything else is relegated to the side. When new vegetarians begin to plan meals, they often feel that there is a great big hole in the center of their plate that needs to be filled with some main dish entrée, usually a high-protein food like beans or cheese. But that is not the way of the world, the rest of the world that is. In other cultures, grains are at the center of the plate. Higher protein foods, such as meat and beans, are used sparingly and are usually incorporated into a sauce that is served over a grain or vegetables. Most of the world's cuisine stresses complex carbohydrates and de-emphasizes protein.

The result is a diet that is high in fiber and low in animal fat. Happily, it is also a diet that makes menu planning simple. As you plan meals, start first with a high-carbohydrate food, such as rice, pasta, and potatoes; and then add lots of vegetables. These foods should nearly fill your plate. Then add smaller amounts of more protein-rich foods, such as legumes and soy products if you like. Toss some toasted nuts into a grain dish or make a simple sauce of black beans with canned diced tomatoes and sautéed onions. Add chunks of marinated tofu to a skewer of fresh diced vegetables and cook over the grill or under the broiler; then serve over a bed of herb-flavored rice.

But every meal does not need to contain these foods. A bowl of vegetable soup with salad and bread is a balanced, nutritious vegetarian meal. A baked potato topped with sautéed vegetables can also be a complete meal. When you realize that every meal does not need to contain a big pile of a "meat alternative," you'll see that vegetarian meal planning becomes very easy.

Some vegetarians include dairy foods and eggs, whereas others eliminate all animal products. We recommend that you aim for minimizing animal foods in your diet. The recipes in this book will help you do this, because they don't include dairy or eggs.

To follow are general guidelines for planning healthful diets.

- *Base diets on whole grains.* These foods are the foundation of healthful diets around the world. Chapter 3 includes instructions for cooking grains. Whenever possible, choose whole, minimally processed grains. That doesn't mean that you have to do this all of the time—just most of the time. To boost your grain intake, build meals around foods like brown rice, quinoa, barley, and pasta. Round out meals with whole grain breads, add grains to soups and stews, and snack on whole grain crackers or popcorn. Enjoy steaming bowls of oatmeal and seven-grain cereal for breakfast. Use whole grains in desserts—try oatmeal cookies, for example.

- *Eat at least four servings of vegetables per day.* This may seem like a lot, but a serving is just one-half cup of cooked vegetable (or one cup of raw). Include a salad at lunch, some raw carrot sticks for a snack, and a cup of steamed or sauteed vegetables at dinner. That's all it takes. But don't be shy about including vegetables at meals. More is better. Studies of different populations show that those who eat more vegetables and fruits have a lower risk of cancer. And vegetables are probably more protective than fruits. In some cultures, vegetables are eaten at breakfast, and there is no reason that you can't do that, too. Keep a supply of washed raw vegetables in plastic bags in your refrigerator, and snack on these during the day; they also travel well as snacks. Toss extra vegetables into any soup or stew. Or mix them into a favorite grain dish. Slice raw and cooked vegetables onto sandwiches.

- Round out your meals with the following:

  - *Fruits:* They are chock-full of many of the same protective factors that we find in vegetables, and they are so easy to add to the diet. Include two to three servings per day. Keep fruit on hand for quick snacks, add them to tossed salads for variety, or toss into curries or other spicy dishes to offer a pleasant cool flavor. Use fruits often in desserts, and add fruit chunks to breakfast cereals.

- *Legumes:* You don't need them at every meal, but you should have them every day. Legumes include all dried beans, peas, and lentils. They also include soy products—tofu, tempeh, soymilk, textured vegetable protein—which are versatile and add variety to many dishes. Make sauces of beans to serve over potatoes and grains, or include beans in soups; pour soymilk over cereal, or use it to make puddings or French toast; make spicy chili or a "meaty" spaghetti sauce with textured vegetable protein (TVP); enjoy tofu on the grill, in a stir-fry, or mashed to make a sandwich spread. You'll be surprised at how easy it is to round out meals with these foods once you experiment with them.

- *Nuts and seeds:* Think these are too fatty to include in your diet? Think again. Yes, nuts and seeds are relatively high-fat foods, but research shows that people who include these foods in their diets actually have a lower risk for heart disease, probably because nuts and seeds provide monounsaturated fats to the diet. A serving of nuts is small (just a couple of tablespoons of chopped nuts or nut butter), and it is true that overdoing it with these foods can add too many calories to your diet. But if you use the condiment approach to eating nuts and seeds— by adding just a few to flavor grain dishes or salads or spread thinly on bread to perk up sandwiches—they become an important part of a healthful diet.

- Be sparing with eggs and dairy if you include them at all. They aren't required for a balanced diet, and they can add unwanted cholesterol and saturated fat. Dairy foods are rich in calcium; but you can also get calcium from many plant foods, which also provide fiber and a lengthy list of compounds that protect against disease.

- Use vegetable oils moderately, but don't eliminate these foods from your diet. How much is too much? We just don't know. Unfortunately, vegetarian diets have come to be equated with very low fat eating over the years, and many vegetarians have proclaimed that eliminating all added fat and high fat foods from the diet is the best bet for optimal health. Neither is necessarily true. Most vegetarians use some oils in cooking and also include higher fat foods, like nuts, seeds, and soy products. And there is evidence that including moderate amounts of certain fats produces better cholesterol levels and better health profiles than do diets that go to great lengths to limit all fats. The key is to choose your fats wisely. Foods high in monounsaturated fats—olives, olive oil, canola oil, avocados, and certain nuts and seeds—have some health benefits. Foods high the fats called omega-3 fatty acids, walnuts, flaxseed, canola oil, and soy products, may also be beneficial. So do limit your fat intake, but don't feel compelled to avoid all fats. A few tablespoons of nuts a day, a serving of soy, and a tablespoon or so of oil can all fit into a healthful diet and may, in fact, be advisable.

The Vegetarian Edge

Looking for reasons to eat more meatless meals? The evidence in favor of a vegetarian diet is overwhelming. A stack of studies shows that vegetarians have lower risk for certain cancers, heart disease, diabetes, hypertension, obesity, gout, and kidney stones.

The reasons are complex. The better health of vegetarians appears to be related to the higher fiber content of the diet and the lower amount of saturated fats and cholesterol. But there is much more about vegetarian diets that appear to be protective. Plant foods are sources of a whole bevy of compounds—some are nutrients and some, called phytochemicals, are not—that may help protect against disease. And animal foods may host compounds that actually raise disease risk. So the shift away from animal foods toward plant foods produces all kinds of beneficial changes in the diet, some of which we are only beginning to understand. Vegetarians have the edge when it comes to good health.

A Few Words about Some Special Nutrients

Calcium

If you minimize or eliminate dairy foods in your diet, you'll need to make sure you are eating other calcium-rich foods. It's not hard to do, but it pays to educate yourself about these foods. The latest recommendations for calcium are high—one thousand milligrams a day for adults and more for older adults—and it's increasingly difficult for people to meet those guidelines, no matter what kind of diet they eat. For adequate calcium, eat generous amounts of calcium-rich foods: leafy, green vegetables; calcium-set tofu (check the label to make sure it contains calcium sulfate); calcium-fortified orange juice; and calcium-fortified soymilk. Some beans and nuts also provide calcium. If you think that your diet falls short of the recommended intake, then use supplements; but use them as added insurance, not as your main source of calcium.

Vitamin B12

Vitamin B12 is found only in animal foods. If you don't eat any animal foods, use a B12 supplement or B12-fortified foods. Many meat analogs, soymilks, and breakfast cereals have B12 added to them. So do some types of nutritional yeast, most notably Red Star brand's Vegetarian Support Formula. Lacto-ovo vegetarians may also not get enough of this nutrient; so it may be wise to use occasional B12 supplements even if you include some dairy and eggs in your diet.

Vitamin D

Vitamin D is poorly supplied in most diets. Eggs and some fish are among the only natural sources of this nutrient. In the United States, milk is fortified with it, but studies show that the actual amount that ends up in milk is variable. Sometimes there is none. Fortunately, we can make all the vitamin D we need from sun exposure: about fifteen minutes of exposure three times a week for light-skinned people and somewhat more for dark-skinned individuals. In northern climates, it's hard to make vitamin D in the winter. It is also difficult for older people to make enough. If you think you might not get enough sun exposure to make vitamin D, then do consider fortified foods (many cereals and some soymilks, for example) or a supplement.

3

A Quick Guide to Vegetarian Foods

A key to putting together great vegetarian meals with little fuss is to always have the basics on hand. Of course, what falls into the category of "basics" is a personal thing. The following list includes both staples and specialty items that are always on our kitchen shelves.

GRAINS

Grains have a long storage life if you keep them cool and dry. Store in airtight containers away from sunlight, and they will last for several months. To avoid bugs, freeze the grains for twenty-four hours when you first bring them home. If you have the space, grains will definitely stay fresher if you can refrigerate or freeze them. See the chart on page 33 for instructions on cooking grains.

The following pages list the grains we use most often in our cooking.

Barley: This is a real old-fashioned grain, often used to make hearty, wintertime vegetable soups. It has a pleasant taste and a wonderful chewy quality. Hulled barley is the whole grain. It's more nutritious than pearled barely but takes a long time to cook. Pearled barley has the fiber-rich bran portion removed but cooks up in about fifteen minutes. Add barley to soups or stews or sauté cooked barley with some onions and mushrooms.

Millet: This tiny, round, yellowish grain is widely used in Asia and Africa. Serve millet with chopped onions and fresh or dried herbs, such as oregano, rosemary, and basil.

Quinoa: Called the Mother Grain by the Incas, this grain was a staple in the diet of that civilization. Always rinse quinoa well before cooking it to remove the soaplike coating that can give it a bitter taste.

Rice: Rice comes in three basic varieties. Long-grain rice is fluffy when cooked and is nice in pilaf. Medium-grain rice is moist and tender right after cooking but becomes sticky as it cools. Short-grain rice is higher in starch and tends to stick together when cooked. It is the traditional rice used in Chinese and Japanese cooking. Within those categories, there are many wonderful types of rice. Here are just a few that you might encounter:

- *Arborio:* A very high starch, short-grain rice used to make risotto, a northern Italian dish that is especially rich and creamy.

- *Basmati:* An aromatic, long-grain rice imported from India and Pakistan. Available as both a brown and white rice.

- *Brown:* The whole rice kernel (with just the outer hull removed). It is available as long-grain, medium-grain, and short-grain varieties and has a nutty flavor and a chewy texture.

- *Japonica:* A Japanese rice that tends to stick together when cooked. It is a good choice for Asian dishes.

- *Jasmine:* An aromatic, long-grain rice imported from Thailand. Try this rice in cold salads, because it stays fluffy even after it has cooled.

- *White:* Polished or milled rice. The bran and germ are both removed so that this rice is slightly more tender than brown rice and cooks more quickly. In the United States, it is nearly always enriched with B vitamins and iron.

- *Wild:* Not really a rice at all and belongs to a completely different family of grasses that grow wild in the lakes of the upper

Midwest and Canada. It is traditionally harvested by hand and is fairly costly. But one cup of wild rice expands to produce four cups of cooked grain.

BEANS

Keep a variety of beans on hand, both canned and dried. Our recipes call mostly for black beans, garbanzos (chickpeas), cannellini beans, and baby limas—our favorite beans. But in any of our recipes, you can substitute your own favorite beans.

Black beans: Natives of the Caribbean and Central and South America, they are wonderful in chili, soups, and spicy dishes.

Black-eyed peas: African slaves brought these beans to the United States, and they have become a much loved ingredient in southern cooking. Good in salads or in spicy bean and grain dishes, they cook quickly and don't require soaking.

Cannellini beans: These white kidney beans are frequently used in Italian dishes. When cooked thoroughly, they have a creamy consistency and can be puréed with herbs, garlic, and lemon to make a nice pâté. Or use them in soups and salads.

Garbanzo beans (also called chickpeas): These are the almost round, light brown salad bar beans. They are very popular in Mediterranean dishes and in Indian cooking. Use them in soups, pasta salads, puréed with tahini and lemon to make the Mid-Eastern staple hummus, and in spicy Indian curries.

Great northern beans: These large white beans have a very mild flavor. Use them for baked beans and in bean soups.

Kidney beans: You can buy both white and red kidney beans. This is the traditional bean called for in most chili recipes.

Lentils: One of the oldest foods known, lentils are used frequently in Mid-Eastern, Mediterranean, and Indian dishes. You'll most likely find brown lentils, but they also come in red and yellow. They cook quickly and don't need to be soaked. Use in lentil soup, Indian dishes, and salads.

Lima beans (also called butter beans): Use either regular or baby limas in soups and stews. They have a rich, deep flavor and are wonderful even with the least amount of seasoning. We much prefer baby limas, which, unfortunately, are not available in canned form.

Navy beans (also called pea beans): These are small white beans that are used in soups and in baked beans.

Pinto beans: These beans are named for their pretty look: a pale beige background with dark brown speckles. A southwestern staple, pintos are used in chili and spicy bean stews.

Soybeans: These are high protein, somewhat high fat beans with a distinct taste, sometimes described as nutty. They need a longer cooking time than other beans and don't have the mild flavor of most beans. We find that they work very well in barbecued bean dishes and other strongly flavored recipes. Look, too, for black soybeans, which have a milder flavor and cook somewhat more quickly.

Split peas: Green or yellow, these are among the fastest cooking of the beans. Use them to make a creamy soup or a sauce for grains and vegetables. They are a staple in Indian cooking and take very well to spicy curry dishes.

Other beans that you can add to your favorite dishes include adzuki, anasazi, appaloosa (brown-and-white speckled), brown beans, cranberry beans, and fava beans.

NUTS, SEEDS, NUT BUTTERS

Fresh nuts and nut butters can go rancid quickly, so store them in the refrigerator. Nuts (but not nut butters) can also be frozen for longer keeping. Nuts can be added to baked goods and grain dishes for extra flavor and crunch. Some good choices to keep on hand are almonds, cashews, hazelnuts, peanuts, pecans, sesame and sunflower seeds, and almond and peanut butters. Here are some nuts and butters that you'll see often in our recipes.

Peanut butter: Buy good, natural peanut butter—freshly ground if possible. It has no added sweeteners or hydrogenated fats, and the texture and flavor are much more appealing than that of processed peanut butter.

Pine nuts (also called pignoli): These tiny nuts have a deep, rich flavor that enlivens any dish. Toast them briefly (just until slightly brown) to bring out their best flavor. Add them to pasta, risotto, and salads.

Tahini: This is roasted sesame seed butter. It is slightly thinner than peanut butter and has a somewhat more bitter taste. With fresh herbs and lemon juice it makes a delightful sauce for grains and vegetables.

SOY FOODS

With the increasing popularity of soy foods, you'll find many of them in your local supermarket. Most are likely to be found in the produce section or in the natural foods section if your store has one. Food co-ops and natural foods stores are also great places to find soy foods.

Soy yogurt: A nondairy yogurt available in a variety of flavors. Like dairy yogurt, this should be refrigerated.

Soy cheese: An imitation cheese made from soybeans. We sometimes use small amounts of grated soy cheese in burritos or on top of chili. Keep soy cheese refrigerated.

Soymilk: The rich liquid expressed from soaked soybeans. It is a wonderful alternative to cow's milk. Most soymilk is in aseptic packages and can be stored at room temperature. Once opened, keep it refrigerated and use within four or five days.

Soy nuts: Roasted soaked soybeans. Great for snacks and salads.

Tempeh: A traditional Indonesian product, this is a cake of fermented soybeans. It has a rich, earthy, mushroomlike flavor. Crumble it with seasonings into sandwich spreads or marinate it and then bake or grill.

Keep tempeh in the freezer for several months or in the refrigerator for four or five days.

Textured vegetable protein (TVP): This is a dehydrated soy protein product. Rehydrate it by pouring seven-eighths cup of boiling water over one cup of dry TVP, and let it sit for five minutes. The texture is similar to cooked ground beef; and it is a wonderful, hearty addition to spaghetti sauce, chili, sloppy Joes, and tacos. Unrehydrated TVP can be stored for several months at room temperature.

Tofu: The curd that results when soymilk is coagulated. Tofu has a mild taste, and it absorbs the flavors of the other ingredients in the recipe, which makes it a very versatile product. You'll find many varieties of tofu, ranging from very firm to soft, silken tofu, which has a custard-like consistency. In our recipes, we specify the type of tofu you should use; it really does make a big difference. It is available in water-filled tubs, which need to be refrigerated, and in aseptic packages that can be stored, unopened, at room temperature. When using firm tofu, be sure to squeeze it between paper towels to get rid of the excess water.

SEA VEGETABLES

You'll find sea vegetables in dried form in natural foods stores and in Asian groceries. Some need to be cooked before they can be eaten. Look for alaria, arame, dulse, hijiki, kombu, nori, and wakame. The sea vegetable we use most often is **kelp powder,** which adds a pleasant, salty flavor to foods. We use it in our mock tuna spread.

DRIED FRUITS

There are many wonderful dried fruits that you can add to grain dishes and salads, including apples, apricots, banana chips, dates, figs, papaya, and peaches. Many of our recipes call for the following:

Currants: These are made from small Zante grapes. Their delicate size and slightly less sweet flavor make them a nice alternative to raisins in dishes. We toss them into green salads and grain dishes.

Raisins: Both dark and golden raisins (the latter are sometimes called sultanas) are available. Some people prefer not to use the golden raisins, because they are treated with sulfur dioxide; but they do have a somewhat juicier flavor that is especially nice in grain dishes. We love raisins in spicy dishes, especially curries.

CONDIMENTS AND SPECIAL INGREDIENTS

Artichokes: These are available canned or frozen and are wonderful in pasta dishes, risotto, and salads.

Capers: Salty, pickled flower buds. Use in bean and grain salads for a wonderful, pungent flavor.

Coconut milk: Canned coconut milk gives dishes, especially curry dishes, a wonderful creaminess and a rich flavor. We always use the light coconut milk, which is much lower in fat than the traditional type.

Eggless mayonnaise: If you avoid eggs, try one of the eggless mayonnaise products. Our favorite is Nayonaise, which is made from tofu.

Fresh garlic: Everyone knows what garlic is, but we've included it in our glossary because we want to make a plea for always using fresh garlic. It takes just an extra minute to mince a clove of garlic, and there is no substitute. Powdered garlic, dried granular garlic, and minced garlic in a jar do not have nearly the same flavor as the real thing.

Fresh gingerroot: Again, opt for fresh if you can. Nothing beats the aroma of sautéed ginger, and it adds a delightful flavor—especially to dishes inspired by Asian cuisine.

Hoison sauce: This sweet Chinese condiment made of soybeans, vinegar, and sweetener gives a wonderful flavor to stir-fries. We also love it in wraps (pages 146–147).

Miso: This is fermented soybean paste and has a wonderful, salty, earthy flavor. It is an essential condiment in Japanese cooking. Use it to make broth for soups and in sauces, stews, grain dishes, and bean dishes.

Mustard: We just love good mustard, especially in salad dressings and sauces. There are many kinds, and it is fun to have a variety to try in different dishes. We consider a good-quality Dijon mustard to be a kitchen staple.

Nutritional yeast: This is an inactive yeast (which means it won't cause bread dough to rise) that is grown on a nutrient-rich culture so that it is usually rich in vitamins. Look for Red Star brand Vegetarian Support Formula, which is rich in vitamin B_{12}.

Olives: Nothing gives life to a platter of pasta or risotto or a green salad like olives. We keep on hand green (stuffed with pimiento), black, and kalamata (purple Greek olives).

Portobello mushrooms: These are actually a giant version of the small brown cremini mushrooms, but the taste of portobellos is much richer. They have been referred to as "vegetarian steak." Grill or broil the whole cap or slice it first and marinate in olive oil, lemon juice, and fresh herbs. Portobellos are expensive but well worth it for a treat.

Salsa: This condiment is enjoying a new image as a trendy food. Traditional salsa is tomato-based and spicy. It is terrific alongside favorite Mexican foods. Newer salsas are made from all types of fruits and vegetables and are enjoyed in a variety of ways. We share a few of our own favorite recipes in Chapter 4.

Shiitake mushrooms: Look for fresh shiitakes, which are getting easier to find. Although these Asian mushrooms are quite pricey, recipes rarely call for more than just a few of them, because their flavor is very intense.

Sun-dried tomatoes: These dried tomatoes are usually bottled in olive oil. You can buy dehydrated ones that need to be soaked in water before using, but we don't recommend them. They never achieve the flavor and texture of their oil-packed counterparts. Sun-dried tomatoes have an exquisite intense flavor that brightens up almost any kind of dish. Chop them and add to risotto, pasta, grain salads, sauces, and spreads.

Tamari: This is real soy sauce that is fermented and aged by traditional methods. It has a much richer taste than commercial soy sauce. Look for it in natural foods stores and Asian markets.

Thai peanut sauce: This is a spicy sauce, so a little goes a long way. Use it condiment-style—that is, use a few tablespoons mixed into a dish, rather than as a sauce served over food. It gives dishes a wonderful flavor boost.

Worcestershire sauce: The traditional kind contains anchovies and, therefore, is not vegetarian. But many brands of light Worcestershire sauce (such as Angostura Lite) are free of anchovies.

VINEGARS

A splash of a good vinegar can brighten up any dish. And it is essential for homemade salad dressings. There is an endless variety to choose from. Apple cider vinegar is useful in bean dishes; but for salads, try raspberry or herb-flavored vinegar. Two types of vinegar that we consider essential are these:

Balsamic vinegar: A Mediterranean vinegar that is slightly sweeter and less acidic than other types. Many cooks swear by the highest quality balsamic vinegar, but it is very expensive. You can find lower priced brands that are quite good.

Rice vinegar: Look for seasoned rice vinegar, which has a somewhat sweet flavor. This Asian condiment has such a mild flavor that we sprinkle it directly on vegetables.

OILS

There are a variety of wonderful oils that add great depth of flavor to cooking. We keep on hand:

Canola oil: This is a good choice when you don't want to taste the oil, because it is mild flavored. We like it because it is rich in healthful monounsaturated fats.

Olive oil: Most of our recipes call for this oil, which has a rich Mediterranean flavor that is essential in many pasta dishes and salads. Do buy good olive oil that is labeled *extra-virgin*. It makes a tremendous difference. Light olive oil is not a substitute for the real thing. It has virtually no flavor. For a real treat, try garlic-, mushroom-, or mustard-infused olive oil.

Sesame oil: This is a good choice for Asian dishes. Use roasted sesame oil for the best flavor.

PASTA

Italian: This is the traditional semolina pasta, made into an endless variety of shapes. Some are available with added vegetables, such as spinach pasta. You can buy whole wheat pasta, which is much higher in fiber than the traditional type. But to be honest, when you eat a vegetarian diet, you can afford to include a few refined grain products in your meals. Let pasta be one of them. The flavor and texture of whole wheat pasta cannot rival the traditional kind.

Asian: These include mung bean noodles, soba noodles (Japanese buckwheat noodles), ramen noodles (Chinese thin, curly soup noodles), and udon (flat, whole wheat noodles).

SWEETENERS

When our recipes call for a sweetener, we usually use either brown sugar or maple syrup. But you can substitute whatever sweetener you have on hand or prefer, with the understanding that the flavor of the dish will be slightly altered. When switching between a dry sweetener and a liquid, you may need to adjust slightly the other liquid called for in the recipe. Some sweetener choices include the following:

Barley malt syrup: This is extracted from sprouted, roasted barley. It's only about half as sweet as sugar but has a pleasant, robust flavor that is nice in baked goods.

Brown sugar: This is white refined sugar that has molasses added to it.

Honey: The flavor of honey varies, depending on the source of the pollen gathered by the bees.

Maple syrup: Pure, rather than maple-flavored, syrup is the concentrated sap of maple trees. It has a distinct flavor that is good in baked products and in baked beans.

Sucanat: This is a brand name for a product made from evaporated and granulated sugarcane juice. Although made from the same plant as white refined sugar, it is a less refined product. Use it in place of granulated sugar, substituting equal amounts of Sucanat for sugar.

White refined sugar: This is common table sugar.

HERBS AND SPICES

Keep dried herbs and spices in tightly sealed bottles or in bags and in a cool, dark cabinet. Although it may be tempting to store your herbs right near the stove, the constant moist heat will cause their flavor and aroma to fizzle. There is no substitute for fresh herbs, and a windowsill garden of a few easy-to-grow favorites (try oregano, thyme, basil, and tarragon) will do much to perk up your dishes. But for convenience sake, we certainly use dried herbs and keep a good supply on hand. Here are a few items that we use frequently but that are not common to all kitchens.

Chinese five-spice powder: This is a blend of cinnamon, cloves, fennel, ginger, and anise (the exact composition of the blend may vary a bit, and it may even contain more than five spices). The flavor is potent, and it adds a nice accent to stir-fries and to baked tofu. Use it sparingly.

Cilantro (also called Chinese parsley): This is the leaf of the coriander plant. It is a potent herb used extensively in Mexican, Indian, and Asian cuisine. This is one of those rare cases in which only the fresh herb can be used; it simply loses all flavor when dried. In fact, it's rare to even find the dried form; but if you do run across it, don't waste your money.

Fennel seeds: These have a licorice-like flavor similar to the spice anise. You can substitute one for the other; but we do prefer fennel, especially in Italian dishes.

Garam masala: This is a blend of spices used frequently in Indian cooking. Like curry blends, recipes for this mix vary among different regions and even different households in India. Garam masalas tend to be slightly sweeter than curries, with an emphasis on spices like cinnamon and cloves.

Mint: This herb, often underused in Western cuisine, adds an appealing freshness to grain dishes and is used extensively in Mid-Eastern dishes. Team it up with couscous and bulgur. Dried mint is a good substitute for fresh; although, as always, fresh is the best choice.

USING CONVENIENCE PRODUCTS

An unfortunate myth in regard to convenience foods is that they sacrifice both nutrition and taste. Admittedly, some processing compromises nutrient content, and some convenience products rely too much on fats, sweeteners, and other ingredients that don't do much to enhance the healthfulness of a meal. But there are plenty of excellent products in your supermarket that are tasty and nutritious and that make fast cooking especially easy without sacrificing flavor or nutrition.

For example, we keep a good supply of canned beans for the times when we can't soak beans ahead of time, or more likely when we've forgotten to do so. Even with the use of a pressure cooker, which speeds bean cookery dramatically, canned beans can come in handy. Vegetarian baked beans can serve as an entrée all alone without any further fixing. Just heat and pour over rice or a baked potato. Or create your own recipe with the addition of your favorite ingredients: stewed tomatoes, sliced vegetarian "hot dogs," or a tablespoon of molasses.

Beans can be used as a staple for making wonderful sauces, soups, and stews. Many are favorites in ethnic cooking, so keeping your shelf stocked with different kinds will expand your culinary horizons and make it easy to prepare your favorite bean dishes. Whether you cook them yourself or used canned, beans have been dried beforehand. They may lose some small amounts of B vitamins, because canning uses high heat; but, generally, canned beans are every bit as nutritious and tasty as the beans you cook yourself.

The same goes for unfairly maligned frozen vegetables. Because they are fast-frozen close to the time of harvest, these products can often be much more nutritious than the "fresh" vegetables that sit on a truck for several days and then in the produce section of your store for several days more.

New convenience products feature whole grains, such as instant soups made with whole grain pasta and instant brown rice. So do take a fresh look at convenience foods. If you choose judiciously and concentrate on the items that fit your cooking style and food preferences, you're likely to find that keeping some of these new convenience products handy on your shelf will let you experiment with fast, healthy, and delicious cooking. One word of warning: Be sure to read the label to make sure the convenience item is truly convenient. Some require the addition of so many ingredients that you might as well start from scratch—and it would be a lot less expensive to do so.

Our Favorite Convenience Foods

Your grocery store is filled with a variety of convenience products. Specialty stores like natural foods stores and ethnic markets have many more. As you experiment with different products, you'll find many that will help you prepare your favorite recipes more quickly and others that encourage you to try new recipes. Here are a few of our favorite convenience products—the items we always keep on our shelves.

Bagged vegetables: Vegetables that are already cut up and washed can save you loads of preparation time. They are certainly much more expensive than their whole counterparts, and we find that they are seldom quite as fresh; but they can be a lifesaver when you are just too busy for the preparation time that fresh vegetables require.

Canned beans (baked beans, refried beans, black, pinto, kidney, garbanzo, white, black-eye peas, limas): You'll note that our recipes often call for either canned or cooked from scratch beans. It's your choice.

Cooking up your own is economical and environmentally sound; but canned beans work great in just about any recipe, and they will save you time. We use both canned and cooked. It depends on how much time we have and whether we remembered to soak the beans!

Canned tomato products: Keep your shelves stocked with stewed tomatoes (look for ones with Mexican, Cajun, and Italian seasonings added), diced and whole tomatoes, and tomato sauce and paste. When there is little to be found for dinner, a can of Italian-flavored stewed tomatoes combined with garbanzo beans, sautéed onions, and a dash of freshly squeezed lemon juice makes a lovely fast sauce to serve over rice or a good thick stew to serve with a loaf of whole grain bread.

Curry paste: Mixed into sautéed vegetables or lentils, these flavorful pastes let you create savory curries in just a few minutes. We prefer the taste of pastes to curry powders. There are several brands of good curry pastes. We like the Patak brand pastes, which are Indian curries—the best. Keep in mind that Thai curry paste tends to be hotter. If you haven't used curry pastes before, do start out with one that is labeled *mild*.

Dried soup mixes: Use these as a flavorful base for your own inventive quick recipes. We add steamed vegetables and canned beans to extend instant soups and turn them into a hearty entrée. Look for brands that are low in sodium.

Frozen vegetables: Frozen vegetables are a nutritious alternative to fresh that will save you cleaning and chopping time. We always keep frozen spinach, corn, and peas as well as various vegetable mixtures on hand and use them to create fast stews and soups.

Hummus mix: Instant hummus (garbanzo bean and sesame butter mix) can't duplicate the flavor of homemade. But it is a good, fast snack for hungry kids and a great item to take along in the car for long trips. Mix it with water and in just a minute or so, you have a dip for pita bread, crackers, or raw vegetables. (We generally cheat a bit and add our own freshly squeezed lemon juice to give the mix a perkier flavor.)

Instant beans (refried, black): These beans are cooked and dried. Just add water to make smooth refried or black beans. Seasoned with salsa, they make a great dip for chips or raw vegetables. Thinned with broth and with the addition of your favorite ingredients (herbs, canned tomatoes, sautéed onions), they are perfect as a soup or sauce for pasta or baked potatoes. These mixes are especially great for travel and camping.

Instant mashed potatoes: The flavor may not rival that of the real thing, but for a fast side dish—or even a quick lunch—instant mashed potatoes can't be beat. They also make a wonderful thickener for soups and can be used as a binder in veggie burgers and loaves. Thinned and added to sautéed onions, they also make good cream of potato soup. See our quick mix for instant cream of potato soup on page 131.

Meat analogs: These are vegetarian products that look and taste like meat. Veggie burgers, "hot dogs," and "sausage" patties and links are among the most popular; and these delicious and super-convenient foods can be found in the freezer section of most supermarkets. Just heat and eat on a bun or crumble them into a soup or stew.

Mexican seasoning: This wonderful blend of spices livens up Mexican dishes. It includes chile peppers, cumin, red pepper, corn flour, salt, and garlic. The flavor can be mild or hot, depending on the brand.

Polenta rolls: These cylinders of firm polenta come in handy for a quick supper or for party appetizers. Just slice, fry, or bake and top with tomato sauce and cooked vegetables. Or layer them in a casserole with spaghetti sauce and vegetables to make polenta lasagna.

Salad dressings: These are so common in most pantries that most of us don't think of them as convenience foods. Truth be told, neither of us buys bottled salad dressing very often. It's such a snap to make your own, and you'll find recipes for very tasty, fast dressings in this book. But sometimes, when you need to have dinner on the table in a big hurry, saving those few minutes can make a difference. The variety of salad dressings on the market is downright staggering, and it can be great fun to try different ones. Using commercial brands allows you to cater to your family's needs and desires as well, because you can choose regular dressings, low-fat varieties, or fat-free ones. Many are delicious tossed with hot steamed vegetables.

Spaghetti sauce: Turn sauce from a jar into your own "homemade" recipe by adding sautéed vegetables, textured vegetable protein, or sliced olives.

Tofu scrambler and tofu seasonings: A variety of products on the market combine seasonings to prepare scrambled tofu or tofu entrées, such as Chinese stir-fry. Just add the mix to cubed or mashed tofu, usually with some water, and heat to prepare delicious tofu breakfasts or dinner entrées.

Vegetable broth: Many of our recipes call for vegetable broth, and the powdered ones and vegetable bouillon cubes are great timesavers. Look for them in the bulk food section of grocery stores and natural foods stores.

How to Cook Grains

Grain (1 cup uncooked)	Liquid (cups)	Cooking Time (minutes)	Yield (cups)
Barley (pearl)	3	50	$3^1/_2$
Bulgur	2	20	3
Couscous (whole wheat or refined)	2	5*	3
Millet	2	25	3
Quinoa	2	15	3
Rice (brown)	2	35–45	3
Rice (refined)	2	20	3

Couscous doesn't require cooking. Bring the water plus 1 tablespoon of oil to a boil. Add the couscous and return to a boil. Remove from the heat immediately; let sit, covered, 5 minutes. Fluff couscous with a fork and it's ready-to-serve.

HOW TO COOK GRAINS

The technique for cooking most grains is basically the same, although the amount of water you use and the cooking time vary.

1. Rinse the grain thoroughly.

2. Measure the liquid into a heavy pot with a tightly fitting lid, and bring the water to a boil. You can also use vegetable broth, or for a lightly sweet flavor, half water and half apple juice. Grains will not cook well in tomato sauce, so add any tomato products after the cooking is completed.

3. Add the grain, return to a boil, then lower to simmer. Cover with the lid, and cook until all the water is absorbed.

4. Most grains will cook best if you add salt after the cooking is completed.

Pressure Cooking Grains

Because some whole grains take a long time to cook, we recommend using a pressure cooker. The cooking procedure is exactly the same; however, the time needed to cook the grain is much less. In some cases, you will use less water, too. When cooking barley, buckwheat, kamut, and oats in the pressure cooker, add several teaspoons of oil to control the foaming.

Pressure Cooking Grains

Grain (1 cup uncooked)	Liquid (cups)	Minutes at High Pressure	Yield (cups)
Barley (pearl)	3	18	3^1/$_2$
Bulgur	1^1/$_2$	6	3
Millet	2	12	3
Quinoa	2	0*	3
Rice (refined)	2	3	2
Rice (brown)	2	15	3

Bring to high pressure; immediately remove from the heat, and allow pressure to reduce naturally.

Toasting Nuts and Seeds

Toasting nuts and seeds brings out their flavor and greatly improves recipes. We especially like to keep toasted pine nuts and sesame seeds on hand for tasty garnishes. Spread them in a single layer on an ungreased cookie sheet, and bake at 325°F until they are lightly browned. Check them frequently, because they can burn very quickly.

Soaking Method 1

1. Place the beans in a large bowl or pot, and add two cups of fresh cold water for each cup of dried beans.

2. Place in the refrigerator, and allow to soak for four to eight hours.

3. Drain the beans thoroughly.

Soaking Method 2

If you suffer from gas when you eat beans, try this soaking technique:

1. Place the rinsed beans in a large pot with three cups of water for each cup of dried beans. Bring to a boil, and boil two minutes. Drain the beans.

2. Add fresh water, again using three cups of water for each cup of beans. Let soak for six hours or more in the refrigerator.

3. Drain the beans, and cook according to the directions given in the chart.

Soaking Method 3: The Quick-Soak Method

If you forgot to soak your beans, try this quick-soak method.

1. Place the beans in a saucepan. Cover them with 2 cups of water for each cup of beans, and bring to a boil.

2. Remove the pan from the heat, cover the pot, and let stand at room temperature for one hour.

Cooking Beans

Beans (1 cup uncooked)	Cooking Time (hours)		Yield (cups)
	Soaked	*Unsoaked*	
Black	$1^1/_2$–2	2–3	2
Black-eyed peas	$^1/_2$	1	2
Cannellini	1–$1^1/_2$	2	2
Garbanzos	2	$3^1/_2$–4	$2^1/_2$
Great northern	$1^1/_2$–2	2–3	2
Kidney	$1^1/_2$	2–3	2
Lentils	*	$^1/_2$–$^3/_4$	2
Baby limas	$^3/_4$–1	$1^1/_2$	2
Navy	$1^1/_2$	$2^1/_2$–3	2
Pinto	$1^1/_2$–2	2–3	2
Soybeans	2–3	3–4	$2^1/_2$
Split peas	*	$^3/_4$	2

*Split peas and lentils do not need to be soaked.

COOKING DRIED BEANS

Be sure to drain the beans well after you have soaked them. Then place them in a large, heavy pot with three cups of water for each cup of soaked beans or four cups water for each cup of unsoaked beans.

Bring the water to a boil. Reduce the heat, cover the pot, and simmer until the beans are tender. Use the chart above to find the approximate cooking times for different varieties of beans.

Pressure Cooking Beans

Because beans require a long cooking time, a pressure cooker is the best way to prepare them. Follow these steps for pressure cooking beans.

1. Use three cups of water for each cup of soaked beans or four cups of water for each cup of unsoaked beans.

2. Add one tablespoon of oil per cup of dried beans if you are using a jiggle-top cooker.

3. Lock the lid in place, bring to high pressure, and cook for the time indicated in the pressure cooking chart.

4. Use a quick-release method of reducing the pressure, according to the manufacturer's instructions.

Pressure Cooking Beans

Beans (1 cup uncooked)	Cooking Time (minutes)		Yield (cups)
	Soaked	*Unsoaked*	
Black	9–11	20–25	2
Black-eyed peas	*	9–11	2
Cannellini	9–12	20–25	2
Garbanzos	10–12	30–40	$2^1/_2$
Great northern	8–12	25–30	2
Kidney	10–12	20–25	2
Lentils	*	7–10	2
Baby limas	5–7	12–15	2
Navy	6–8	15–25	2
Pinto	4–6	22–25	2
Soybeans	9–12	25–35	$2^1/_2$
Split peas	*	8–10	2

Black-eyed peas, lentils, and split peas do not need to be soaked.

4

Quick-and-Easy Vegetarian Recipes

ABOUT OUR RECIPES

We don't promise dinner on the table in fifteen minutes, although many of our recipes will let you achieve just that. Others require a little cooking time. The actual hands-on preparation is fast and easy for all of our recipes, though. We've also tried to keep preparation uncomplicated so that you won't have a sink full of pots and pans to wash when you are finished. Don't shy away from recipes just because the list of ingredients looks a little long. In our recipes, many of the ingredients are simple additions that don't require any chopping or extra preparation. Adding three or four spices takes you just about a minute but reaps big rewards in terms of flavor.

Keep in mind that all recipes take a little longer than normal the first time you make them. Once you have prepared a dish several times and the recipe is familiar, you'll find that the preparation time shortens.

Several of the recipes in this book are prizewinners from a contest for quick vegetarian recipes that was sponsored by the Physicians Committee for Responsible Medicine, a health promotion organization that advocates vegetarian diets. They are some of the tastiest vegetarian dishes we've eaten.

As you experiment with new recipes, don't be afraid to be creative. If a recipe calls for an ingredient that you don't have or that isn't a favorite with your family, substitute with whatever works for your cooking style. If you don't like black-eyed peas, you can still enjoy our Mediterranean Black-Eyed Pea Salad. Just substitute great northern beans or kidney beans or whatever strikes your fancy. Substitute quinoa or wheat berries or barley in any recipe that calls for rice. Or you might even let pasta fill in for the grain in a stew or salad. If you don't cook with wine, substitute freshly squeezed lemon juice or vegetable broth. If a recipe calls for zucchini but green beans were on sale this week, make the switch. Your creative touches will make the recipes your own.

DO YOU REALLY NEED A RECIPE?

It's always fun to discover a great new recipe and add it to one's repertoire of family favorites. But most of the time, most of us don't cook from recipes. Fast cooking often means whipping up dishes that are so familiar and easy to prepare that we don't need recipes. That's the way many busy cooks get dinner on the table, vegetarian or not. Although we hope that you'll find the recipes in this book fun and useful, we also know that most vegetarian cooks don't have the leisure to follow a recipe every night. What can you put on the table that doesn't require any reading and measuring but that constitutes a tasty and nutritious dinner? Here are a few ideas:

- Veggie burgers on whole wheat rolls, fresh or frozen steamed vegetables, instant mashed potatoes or microwaved baked potatoes.

- Spaghetti with sauce from a jar, salad, whole wheat bread.

- Baked potatoes, canned vegetarian beans, steamed vegetables, salad.

- Canned or instant soup, salad, whole wheat rolls.

- Homemade burritos made with canned or instant refried beans, shredded soy cheese, chopped tomatoes, and lettuce.

- Impromptu vegetable soup, using whatever happens to be in the refrigerator or freezer. Sauté onions and garlic, add chunks of any vegetables that strike your fancy, pour in vegetable broth and perhaps a can or two of diced tomatoes, and add your favorite herbs. Serve with rice or pasta to make a more filling soup.

For other ideas for putting together tasty, nutritious meals without consulting a cookbook, see the discussions about wraps (pages 146–147) and gourmet leftovers (pages 148–149).

FRESH SIMPLICITY

It's not always possible to cook with fresh ingredients. Some ingredients are not available year-round or are prohibitively expensive and not terribly flavorful out of season. And using fresh foods takes more time. Certainly, it takes longer to chop up fresh parsley than it does to add a few pinches of dried. But you will also find that fresh foods often do lend themselves to fast, convenient cooking. This is because they are so flavorful that they beg to be used in the most simple of dishes, in which the taste of a few fresh ingredients make laborious preparation and long lists of ingredients unnecessary.

In Italy, home to some of the finest vegetarian cooking in the world, often the best dishes are also the least complicated. The ingredients themselves are so special that good dishes are almost guaranteed. Pasta might be tossed with garlic, fresh ripe tomatoes, and an abundance of basil straight from the kitchen garden.

If you have a home garden, you know that a summer meal consisting of a big platter of herbed, sautéed homegrown vegetables, perhaps with a loaf of fresh bread, is enough. The straight-from-the-garden taste is so wonderful that nothing else is needed to make this a feast. Or cubed boiled potatoes, tossed with fresh basil, corn right off the cob from a roadside stand, and a sprinkling of good olive oil, vinegar, and salt is a gourmet meal that doesn't require a recipe. Sure, it takes a little bit of time to shuck the corn, boil it, and then slice the kernels from the cob. But that's more or less the extent of dinner preparation. Serve your impromptu potato salad with sliced tomatoes and some bread.

Although you won't always be able to serve such delectable meals from fresh ingredients, when you do have these wonderful foods at your disposal, don't shy away from them because of preparation time. Just remember that when your ingredients are wonderful, it takes almost no effort to turn them into a meal—and yourself into a gourmet cook.

HOW WE COOK

My kitchen bookshelves house more than seventy vegetarian cookbooks. Although I have used and continue to use most of them at one time or another, my weekly menus tend to revolve around the same dozen or so favorite recipes.

It turns out that I am quite typical in this regard. Most Americans have a limited repertoire of tried-and-true favorite meals—just ten to twelve meals for the average family—and they eat these over and over again. If you think back on your childhood, chances are that this is the way your mother cooked, too. If you are just starting out as a vegetarian cook, this is rather reassuring. It means that it's really quite easy to adopt a vegetarian diet. All it takes is finding ten to twelve recipes that you enjoy and feel comfortable preparing. Because the recipes here are super easy, you'll find this book a great place to start.

Of course, as you become more familiar with vegetarian foods, you'll probably add new recipes. I find that my menus are fairly flexible over time. That is, periodically I'll try a new recipe, and it quickly becomes a favorite that I make several times a month. At the same time, I might get tired of preparing and eating old favorites, and they get retired. But rest assured that even cookbook authors are likely to make the same recipes over and over again.

Grains and Beans

Buttery Beans with Mushrooms

Makes 6 servings

Baby lima beans deserve their nickname of "butter beans." They have a rich, buttery flavor without the fat. This is one instance when we think cooking your own rather than using canned makes a big difference. Canned limas are larger and have a grainier texture than freshly cooked bean. Soaked baby limas take just 10 minutes to cook in the pressure cooker.

3 tablespoons olive oil

1 small onion, coarsely chopped

1 clove garlic, minced

1 stalk celery, chopped

2 cups sliced mushrooms

1^1/$_2$ cups cooked baby limas with ^{1}/$_2$ cup cooking liquid or one (15.5-ounce) can, undrained

1 teaspoon dried tarragon

Salt and freshly ground black pepper to taste

In a large skillet, heat oil over medium heat, and add onion, garlic, celery, and mushrooms. Sauté until tender, about 8 minutes. Add beans and tarragon, and simmer 15 to 30 minutes. Season with salt and pepper.

Beans and Apples

Makes 6 servings

The combination of beans, apples, and vegetarian "sausage" gives this dish a pleasant sweet-and-spicy flavor. It is simply wonderful served over a grain or with roasted potatoes and steamed vegetables.

2 tablespoons olive oil

2 medium onions, thinly sliced

2 cloves garlic, minced

1/2 pound vegetarian "sausage," crumbled into coarse bits

1 1/2 cups tomato juice

1/2 cup firmly packed light brown sugar

1/4 teaspoon chili powder

One (15-ounce) can small red or white beans or 2 cups cooked

2 apples, thinly sliced*

Salt and freshly ground black pepper to taste

In a large, deep skillet, heat oil over medium heat, and sauté onions and garlic until onions are tender, about 8 minutes. Add the "sausages" and sauté for 2 minutes more. Add the remaining ingredients. Simmer, covered, until apples are tender, about 10 minutes.

Peel the apples if you'd like, but it isn't necessary.

Tips and Variations

Substitute spicy vegetable cocktail juice for the tomato juice and skip the chili powder if you'd like.

Southern-Style Ranch Beans

Makes 8 servings

This super-fast bean dish makes enough for a crowd. Serve it over quinoa or rice or on the side with a baked potato. If you like your beans less sweet, use the smaller amount of brown sugar. See our Planover recipe for Mexican-Style Baked Beans (page 166) for a slightly spicier version of this dish.

2 tablespoons oil

2 medium onions, chopped

$^1/_4$ to $^1/_2$ cup firmly packed brown sugar

2 tablespoons prepared mustard

1 tablespoon cider vinegar

One (15-ounce) can pinto beans or 2 cups cooked

One (28-ounce) can vege- tarian baked beans

One (14.5-ounce) can stewed tomatoes

In a large saucepan, heat the oil over medium heat, and sauté onions until tender, about 8 minutes. Stir in the remaining ingredients. Simmer, covered, 20 minutes.

Sweet-and-Sour Red Cabbage with Beans

Makes 4 servings

Beans teamed up with sweet-and-sour cabbage make a delicious and hearty meal for a winter evening. Or serve it at room temperature for a summer buffet or picnic. You can substitute any beans you like, but beware that white beans—such as baby limas and great northerns—will take on an unusual magenta hue in this dish!

3 tablespoons canola oil

3 tablespoons minced onion

4 cups red cabbage, shredded

1/4 cup dry white wine

3 tablespoons white vinegar

5 teaspoons firmly packed light brown sugar

1/4 teaspoon freshly ground black pepper

One (15-ounce) can red kidney or pinto beans or 2 cups cooked

In a large saucepan, heat the oil over medium heat, and sauté onion and cabbage until cabbage wilts, about 8 minutes. Add the remaining ingredients. Simmer, covered, stirring occasionally, 30 to 40 minutes.

Hoppin' José

Makes 4 servings

Here is a south-of-the-border twist to the old southern favorite Hoppin' John. It takes just a few minutes to prepare if you have some leftover cooked rice on hand—or use instant brown rice. Evelyn Wootton of Port Ludlow, Washington, sent us this recipe. You can bake this in a conventional oven or in the microwave.

One (15-ounce) can black beans, drained, or 2 cups cooked, drained

2 cups cooked brown or white rice

$1/2$ cup finely chopped mild red onion

1 cup medium salsa

One (4-ounce) can diced green chiles or $1/4$ cup diced fresh

$1/2$ cup chopped scallions (green onions), including green portion

Preheat oven to 350°F, if using.

In a medium bowl, toss beans, rice, red onion, salsa, and chiles. Place in a 1-quart ovenproof or microwavable casserole. Bake 25 minutes or microwave on high 2 to 3 minutes. Top with scallions just before serving.

Creamy Curried Garbanzo Beans and Spinach

Makes 4 servings

Coconut milk plus curry paste produces a creamy and savory dish that tastes as though it must have taken hours to prepare. But this wonderful Indian recipe comes together in just a few minutes. Add your own touches if you'd like: frozen green peas instead of spinach or cubes of cooked potatoes instead of garbanzo beans.

2 tablespoons vegetable oil

1 medium onion, coarsely chopped

3 cloves garlic, minced

2 medium thin-skinned potatoes (try yellow Finns), cut in 1/2-inch cubes

1/2 cup water

1 tablespoon curry paste or 2 teaspoons powder

One (14-ounce) can light coconut milk

One (15-ounce) can garbanzo beans (chickpeas) or 2 cups cooked

1 cup tightly packed thawed, frozen chopped spinach

One-half (14.5 ounce) can diced tomatoes or 1 medium fresh tomato, diced

2 tablespoons sugar

Salt to taste

4 cups cooked brown rice

In a large saucepan, heat oil over medium heat, and sauté onions until tender, about 8 minutes. Add garlic, and sauté 1 minute. Add potatoes, water, and curry paste; simmer 10 minutes. Add coconut milk, garbanzo beans, and spinach; simmer 5 minutes. Add tomatoes and sugar, stirring to combine well, and cook until heated through. Add salt to taste. Serve over brown rice.

Tips and Variations

Coconut milk is high in saturated fat. Be sure to use light coconut milk, which is much lower in fat.

Baked Five-Spice Tofu

Makes 4 servings

Baked tofu is wonderful in sandwiches or added to grain dishes. This also makes a nice appetizer, skewered on toothpicks and served with one of our sauces for dipping. This marinade is very simple but produces a big flavor. It is best if you allow the tofu to marinate for a bit, so try preparing this dish a day ahead or early in the day for dinner in the evening.

1 pound firm tofu

$^1/_3$ cup soy sauce

1 tablespoon water

1 tablespoon pure maple syrup

1 tablespoon minced ginger-root

1 teaspoon curry powder or 1 tablespoon paste

$^1/_2$ teaspoon five-spice powder

Cut the tofu into $^1/_2$-inch cubes, and place in a casserole. In a small bowl, whisk together the remaining ingredients, and pour over tofu. If time allows, marinate tofu (in the refrigerator) for at least 1 hour.

Preheat oven to 350°F. Cover the casserole, and bake 30 minutes. Uncover, and bake 20 minutes more.

Tofu Corn Puffs

Makes 8 croquettes

These croquettes are light as a feather and delicious. This is a tried-and-true way to introduce tofu to your family. You can serve them sandwich-style in a bun, but they are fairly delicate and soft, so we prefer to eat them with a fork.

$1/2$ **cup cashews**

$1/2$ **cup water**

8 ounces soft tofu

2 tablespoons nutritional yeast

1 medium onion, finely chopped

2 cups frozen corn kernels, thawed

$1/2$ **teaspoon dried basil or 1 tablespoon chopped fresh**

2 cups soft bread crumbs

Vegetable oil for frying

Put cashews and water in the bowl of a food processor fitted with the steel blade; process until cashews are completely puréed. Add tofu and yeast, and blend until puréed. Scrape mixture into a medium bowl, and stir in onion, corn, basil, and bread crumbs. Form into patties.

Cook them as you would a burger: In a large frying pan, heat a small amount of oil; sauté patties until brown.

Tips and Variations

Soft bread crumbs are better than dried ones in this recipe. Whenever you have some ends of bread left over, toss them into your food processor, and process into crumbs. Then store in a plastic bag in the freezer, and you will have a good supply of fresh bread crumbs whenever you need them.

Quick-and-Easy Vegetable Quinoa with Tahini Sauce

Makes 4 servings

Turnips are an unusual addition to this dish; we love the flavor they add.

2 cups vegetable broth

1 zucchini cut in half lengthwise, then into $1/4$-inch slices

1 or 2 carrots cut in 1-inch lengths

1 medium turnip cut in $1/2$-inch cubes

$1/2$ red bell pepper cut in strips

1 cup quinoa, rinsed and drained

Lemon Tahini Sauce (page 108)

One (15-ounce) can garbanzo beans (chickpeas), drained, or 2 cups cooked, drained

1 teaspoon ground cumin

$1/8$ to $1/4$ teaspoon cinnamon

Freshly squeezed lime juice to taste (optional)

In a medium saucepan, heat vegetable broth to a boil. Add all vegetables, reduce heat, and simmer about 3 minutes. Add quinoa, and simmer until broth is absorbed, about 15 minutes.

Meanwhile, make the Lemon Tahini Sauce; set aside.

Stir garbanzo beans and spices into the quinoa mixture. Let sit a few minutes; then fluff with a fork, and serve. Top with a squeeze of lime juice, if desired, and some Lemon Tahini Sauce.

Tips and Variations

Be sure to rinse the quinoa well before cooking.

Any leftovers are great served in a pita pocket and topped with more Lemon Tahini Sauce.

Quinoa with Corn and Beans

Makes 4 servings

Although quinoa is indigenous to the Andes Mountains—an elevation too high to grow corn—the flavors of quinoa and corn seem made for each other. Use any type of bean that you like; we love small seasoned white beans in this dish.

2 tablespoons olive oil

1 onion, coarsely chopped

2 cloves garlic, minced

2 cups vegetable broth

1 cup quinoa, rinsed

1¹/₂ cups frozen corn kernels

One (15-ounce) can beans or 2 cups cooked

¹/₂ teaspoon dried oregano

¹/₂ teaspoon dried tarragon

Salt to taste

In a large, deep skillet heat the oil over medium heat, and sauté onion and garlic about 3 minutes. Add vegetable broth, and bring to a boil. Add quinoa, reduce heat to a simmer, cover, and cook until broth is absorbed, 15 to 20 minutes. Add corn, beans, herbs, and salt tossing to mix. Cook over very low heat until the corn is hot, 3 minutes.

Tips and Variations

For a delicious variation—and a very traditional combination—replace the beans in this recipe with 1¹/₂ cups cooked diced potatoes.

Curried Rice with Raisins and Vegetables

Makes 4 servings

This rice dish can be a quick-and-easy side dish or a more complete meal with the addition of baked tofu, more vegetables, or a can of garbanzo beans. The raisins give it a pleasing sweet taste.

2 cups water

1 cup basmati or plain white rice

1 to 2 tablespoons curry paste

$1/2$ cup frozen green peas

$1/2$ cup frozen sweet yellow or white corn

$1/4$ cup golden raisins or currants

In a large saucepan, bring water to a boil, add rice. Reduce heat; simmer, covered, 15 minutes. Stir in curry paste, vegetables, and raisins. Continue cooking, covered, 5 minutes more. Remove from heat, and let sit several minutes. Fluff with a fork before serving.

Curried Vegetables with Basmati Rice

Makes 4 servings

Some of our favorite recipes come from India. The variety of vegetable and rice entrées seems endless. For most Indian food, the sauce makes the dish; but usually their complex blend of spices and flavors are too time-consuming to be considered a quick fix. Using a commercial Indian sauce, like the Patak brand Dopiaza sauce or Taj Gourmet Simmer Sauce, makes it easy to create a wonderful authentic taste. Try other Indian sauces with this recipe as well.

2 thin-skinned potatoes cut into $^1/_2$-inch cubes

One (15-ounce) jar Patak brand Dopiaza Mild Cooking Sauce

$^1/_2$ cup water

One (15-ounce) can garbanzo beans (chickpeas), drained, 2 cups cooked, drained

1 cup frozen peas

Vegetable broth (optional)

3 cups cooked basmati or jasmine rice

Chutney (mango or other)

In a medium saucepan, cover potatoes with water. Bring to a boil, and boil gently until tender, about 10 minutes. Drain, and return potatoes to saucepan. Add Dopiaza sauce, water, garbanzo beans, and peas. Cook just until the peas are defrosted, 2 minutes. Dilute the sauce with vegetable broth or more water if it is too thick. Serve with rice and chutney.

Tips and Variations

Instead of peas, substitute one (10-ounce) package of frozen spinach, cooked briefly and drained.

Brown Rice with Spicy Red Sauce and Harvest of Veggies

Makes 6 servings

This recipe was inspired by a teen's need for a filling vegetarian meal when there's very little to work with. The result is a dish that is hearty and tasty and fun to make. This recipe was a prizewinner in the Physicians Committee for Responsible Medicine recipe contest and was sent to us by Danny Seo of Shillington, Pennsylvania. Serve it with a big platter of steamed vegetables for a very filling meal.

1 tablespoon olive oil

$^{1}/_{2}$ cup coarsely chopped onion

1 frozen veggie burger, thawed

6 medium mushrooms cut into fourths

One (15-ounce) can garbanzo beans (chickpeas), drained, or 2 cups cooked, drained

1 cup frozen corn kernels

$^{3}/_{4}$ cup tomato salsa

Pinch dried red pepper flakes

Freshly ground black pepper to taste

Pinch salt

3 cups cooked brown rice

In a large saucepan, heat olive oil over medium heat, and add onion. Crumble veggie burger into small pieces (resembling ground beef) and add to pan. Cook until onions are transparent and veggie burger is brown, about 8 minutes. Add mushrooms. Cover, and cook 1 minute. Add the garbanzo beans, corn, salsa, red pepper flakes, black pepper, and salt. Cook 1 to 2 minutes more. Add brown rice, and toss until hot and well mixed.

Tips and Variations

This is the perfect recipe for using up leftovers. Any veggie burger works fine, and you can substitute other beans and grains as well.

Instant Brown Rice with Tomato Pesto, Zucchini, and Red Pepper

Makes 4 servings

Sun-dried tomato pesto can be found in many specialty food stores or gourmet groceries. Although expensive, a little goes a long way and keeps for several weeks in your refrigerator. To make your own, see page 104. (Our recipe is super fast.) We just love the idea of tossing a small amount of pesto (this recipe uses just 2 tablespoons) with fresh vegetables and then serving them over a grain. Try it with orzo for a real treat. Here we've teamed the vegetables with instant brown rice, a good fast-cooking version of the whole grain.

2 teaspoons olive oil

1/2 medium onion, sliced

4 small or 3 large zucchini, cut in half lengthwise and then in 1/4-inch slices

1/2 red bell pepper cut in 1/4-inch slices

2 tablespoons prepared sun-dried tomato pesto or homemade

4 cups cooked instant brown rice

In a large saucepan, heat oil over medium heat, and sauté onion 3 to 5 minutes. Add zucchini, bell pepper, and pesto. Stir-fry until tender–crisp, about 5 minutes. Serve over brown rice.

Two Wonderful Risotto Dishes for the Pressure Cooker

Risotto is made with very short-grain arborio rice, which is popular in Italy. Traditional preparation requires slow cooking and constant stirring and is much too fussy for anything but a special occasion. We are grateful to vegetarian cookbook author Lorna Sass for introducing us to risotto made in the pressure cooker. It cooks up quickly and produces the wonderful creamy consistency that is the hallmark of good risotto—with almost no effort at all.

Risotto with White Beans and Olives

Makes 4 servings

2 tablespoons olive oil

1 cup coarsely chopped onions

2 cloves garlic, minced

1^1/$_2$ cup arborio rice

3^1/$_2$ cups vegetable broth

1 teaspoon dried oregano

^{1}/$_2$ teaspoon dried basil

^{1}/$_2$ teaspoon salt

1 cup packed baby spinach leaves

^{1}/$_4$ cup sliced black olives

One (15-ounce) can small white seasoned beans, drained

In a pressure cooker, heat oil over medium heat, and sauté onions and garlic until onions are soft but not brown. Add rice, stir until golden, 1 to 2 minutes. Immediately add broth, oregano, basil, and salt. Lock lid in place, and bring cooker to high pressure; cook 5 minutes. Use a quick-release method of reducing the pressure, according to the manufacturer's instructions. Remove lid, and stir in the remaining ingredients. Cook, stirring, over low heat until the spinach is wilted, about 2 minutes.

Mushroom Risotto with Sun-Dried Tomatoes and Artichokes

Makes 4 servings

1 tablespoon olive oil

1 medium onion, finally chopped

1 cup arborio rice

1 1/2 cups chopped fresh mushrooms*

2 cups vegetable or vegetarian chicken-flavored broth

1/4 cup dry white wine

1/4 cup oil-cured sun-dried tomatoes, snipped into small pieces

One (9-ounce) package frozen artichoke hearts

1 teaspoon dried herbes de Provence or mixed dried Italian herbs

Salt and freshly ground black pepper to taste

In a 2 quart or larger pressure cooker, heat oil over medium high heat and sauté onion until translucent, 5 minutes. Add rice, and stir until golden, 1 to 2 minutes. Add mushrooms, and stir to mix. Add broth, wine, tomatoes, artichoke hearts, herbs, salt and pepper; stir until mixture comes to a boil. Lock lid in place, and bring cooker to low pressure; cook 7 minutes. Use a quick-release method of reducing the pressure, according to the manufacturer's instructions. Remove lid, and stir gently before serving.

Use firm brown or white mushrooms; a few fresh shiitake mushrooms will provide additional flavor.

Couscous with Carrots and Garbanzo Beans

Makes 4 servings

Couscous cooks in just a few minutes, and its delicate flavor quickly absorbs sauces and spices. We like whole wheat couscous, which seems to have more flavor and a slightly crunchier texture than the regular kind. This dish is especially tasty served with Lemon or Orange Tahini Sauce (pages 108–109).

$1^1/_2$ cups vegetable broth

2 tablespoons olive oil

1 cup whole wheat or refined couscous

$^1/_2$ onion, sliced

1 clove garlic minced or 1 teaspoon garlic-infused olive oil

2 carrots, sliced

One (15-ounce) can garbanzo beans (chickpeas), drained, or 2 cups cooked, drained

$^1/_2$ to 1 red bell pepper, sliced

1 teaspoon salt

1 to 2 teaspoons dried dill

$^1/_4$ cup currants or raisins

1 to 2 teaspoons freshly snipped mint leaves (optional)

$^1/_4$ cup toasted pine nuts (optional)

In a medium saucepan, bring broth and 1 tablespoon of oil to a boil. Add couscous, and return to a boil. Remove immediately from heat, cover, and let sit 5 minutes.

Meanwhile, in a large saucepan, heat the remaining 1 tablespoon oil over medium heat, and sauté onion, garlic and carrots, until onion is translucent, about 4 minutes. Add garbanzo beans, bell pepper, salt, and dill; cook, covered, 5 minutes. Remove from heat, and stir in currants and mint, if desired.

To serve, fluff couscous with a fork and mound on a platter. Top with vegetables, and garnish with pine nuts, if desired.

Sloppy Joes

Makes 4 servings

Homemade sloppy Joes are an old-time favorite, especially nice for a winter weekend supper. This is an easy vegetarian version.

1¹/₄ cups boiling water

1¹/₂ cups textured vegetable protein

1 tablespoon canola oil

¹/₂ cup coarsely chopped onion

¹/₂ cup coarsely chopped green bell pepper

Two (15-ounce) cans tomato sauce

1 tablespoon chili powder plus more to taste

1 tablespoon prepared mustard

2 tablespoons sugar

Tamari to taste

4 hamburger rolls

In a small bowl, pour water over textured vegetable protein. Let stand until rehydrated, 5 minutes. In a large saucepan, heat oil over medium heat, and sauté onion and bell pepper until tender, about 8 minutes. Add textured vegetable protein, tomato sauce, chili powder, mustard, and sugar. Simmer 10 minutes. Add tamari and more chili powder, if desired. Serve over rolls.

The Best and Fastest Chili

Makes 6 servings

This chili always pleases even the most dedicated meat-eater. Most people can't tell the difference. We're grateful to Neal Barnard, M.D., president of the Physicians Committee for Responsible Medicine, for sharing this recipe with us.

$^{7}/_{8}$ **cup boiling water**

1 cup textured vegetable protein

1 tablespoon canola oil

1 onion, coarsely chopped

1 green bell pepper, diced

2 tablespoons chili powder

2 teaspoons ground cumin

2 teaspoons garlic powder

1 teaspoon dried oregano

$^{1}/_{4}$ **teaspoon allspice**

Two (15-ounce) cans diced tomatoes

One (15-ounce) can pinto, kidney, or black beans

One (3-ounce) can tomato paste

One (2-ounce) can diced jalapeño chile

In a small bowl, pour water over textured vegetable protein; Set aside. In a large skillet, heat oil over medium heat, and sauté onion and bell pepper until tender, about 8 minutes. Add the textured vegetable protein and the remaining ingredients; mix thoroughly. Simmer 30 minutes. Serve alone or over a cooked grain of your choice.

Pasta Recipes

Thai Pasta with Broccoli and Coconut Milk

Makes 4 servings

This exotic, but easy to prepare, recipe was a grand-prize winner in the Physicians Committee for Responsible Medicine recipe contest. It was sent to us by Kimberly Erickson of Santa Rosa, California. We've made the recipe especially simple and fast by including just one vegetable: broccoli. You can use a combination of your favorite vegetables if you'd like. Try red bell peppers, potatoes, carrots, asparagus, green beans, or sweet onions.

1 pound uncooked small pasta (penne, bow-ties)

3 cups broccoli florets

1/4 cup packed fresh basil leaves

2 tablespoons soy sauce

1 tablespoon mild curry paste or 2 teaspoons powder

1 tablespoon vegetable oil

1 teaspoon sugar

1/2 teaspoon turmeric

2 cloves garlic, minced

One (14-ounce) can light coconut milk

Cook pasta according to package directions. At the same time, steam broccoli until just tender.

Meanwhile, combine the remaining ingredients in the container of a blender. Blend to mix thoroughly.

Drain pasta and toss with broccoli. Spoon coconut milk sauce over top.

Spiced Tofu and Pasta

Makes 4 servings

This delicious pasta dish, adapted from a shrimp recipe, takes just minutes to prepare and is fun to serve for an informal company dinner. Try it with steamed asparagus or baby greens salad and a loaf of crusty French bread.

1 tablespoon soy sauce

1 teaspoon five-spice powder

1 to 2 tablespoons minced gingerroot

12 to 14 ounces firm tofu, cut into $1/2$-inch cubes

1 large clove garlic, minced

$1/2$ cup freshly squeezed orange juice

1 tablespoon rice vinegar

2 teaspoons honey mustard

Dash cayenne or hot sauce to taste

1 pound uncooked fresh linguine or 12 ounces dried

1 tablespoon olive oil

1 teaspoon roasted sesame oil (optional)

1 bunch (about 6) scallions (green onions), thinly sliced, including about $1/2$ cup green portion (optional)

In a large saucepan, heat water to a boil to cook the pasta. Meanwhile, in a small bowl, whisk together soy sauce, five-spice powder, cornstarch (optional, see tip below), and ginger. Pour over tofu and let marinate while you prepare the remaining ingredients.

In a medium saucepan, combine garlic, orange juice, vinegar, mustard, and cayenne. Add marinated tofu, and simmer 2 to 3 minutes. Meanwhile, cook pasta in the boiling water, according to package directions. Drain pasta, and toss with olive oil and sesame oil, if desired. Top with tofu mixture and garnish with scallions, if desired.

Tips and Variations

Fresh pasta is especially wonderful with this dish.

If you would like a thicker sauce, whisk together 1 teaspoon cornstarch and 3 tablespoons water. Add to sauce, and simmer for several minutes to thicken.

Ramen Noodles with Vegetables and Roasted Sesame Oil

Makes 4 servings

It's easy to make a fast pasta and vegetable dish when you begin with fast-cooking ramen noodles and add your own vegetables. This recipe is ready in less than 5 minutes. The dash of dark roasted sesame oil makes it especially tasty.

4 cups water

2 packages vegetable or mushroom ramen noodles with seasoning packets

$^1/_2$ to 1 cup frozen green peas

$^1/_2$ to 1 cup frozen sweet yellow or white corn

1 teaspoon dark sesame oil

1 tablespoon toasted sesame seeds

1 bunch (about 6) scallions (green onions), thinly sliced, including green portion (optional)

In a medium saucepan, bring water to a boil, and add noodles. Boil 3 minutes. Add vegetables, return to a boil, immediately remove from heat. Drain. Stir in contents of seasoning packets, and mix in sesame oil. Top each serving with sesame seeds and chopped scallions, if desired.

Tips and Variations

You can also serve this dish as a soup if you don't drain the liquid after cooking the noodles and vegetables. Other vegetables that are delicious additions are broccoli florets, green beans, and asparagus. You can also add cubes of tofu.

Hot Baba Ghanoush with Pasta

Makes 4 servings

This unusual pasta recipe is a hit with eggplant lovers. You'll need a little extra time to make this, because the eggplant requires 40 minutes to bake. We suggest baking it ahead of time, and then putting the recipe together the next day. It can be served as a sauce, a dip for fresh vegetables, or as a spread for French bread.

2 small or 1 large eggplant

$1/2$ teaspoon salt plus additional for eggplant

One-half (10-ounce) package soft silken tofu

2 tablespoons tahini

$1/4$ cup dry sherry, dry white wine, or vegetable broth

$1/4$ cup freshly squeezed lemon juice

Grated rind from 1 lemon

3 cloves garlic, coarsely chopped

1 tablespoon olive oil

$1/8$ to $1/4$ teaspoon cayenne

1 pound uncooked small pasta (spirals, small shells, penne)

$1/4$ cup chopped fresh parsley for garnish

Preheat oven to 400°F. Lightly oil a baking sheet.

Cut eggplant in half, sprinkle the flesh with salt and let sit a half hour. Pat dry, and place cut side down on prepared sheet. Pierce with fork several times; then bake 40 minutes, or until very soft. When cool, scoop out the insides into the container of a food processor fitted with the steel blade or a blender. Add $1/2$ teaspoon salt and the remaining ingredients except pasta and parsley; purée. Let sit at least 15 minutes to allow flavors to blend.

Cook pasta according to package directions. Meanwhile, heat eggplant mixture over low heat. Drain pasta, and toss with sauce. Garnish with parsley.

Tips and Variations

You can use either soft or firm silken tofu in this dish, but don't use the low-fat and extra-firm varieties, because they will not produce as creamy a sauce.

Pasta with Eggplant and Mushrooms

Makes 4 servings

This is a wonderful way to turn your favorite jar of spaghetti sauce into something with a homemade taste. Chunky and rich, this sauce is simple to make.

2 pounds eggplant (1 large or 2 small)

Salt

4 tablespoons olive oil

3 cloves garlic, minced

1 pound firm fresh mushrooms, thinly sliced

1 pound uncooked pasta

One (32-ounce) jar meatless spaghetti sauce

Slice skin off eggplant, and cut flesh into $^1/_2$-inch cubes. Place in a colander, salt lightly, and set aside while you prepare the rest of the vegetables.

In a large saucepan, heat the oil over medium heat, and sauté eggplant and minced garlic 1 to 2 minutes. It will immediately soak up most of the oil. Add mushrooms, and stir to combine. Cover, and cook until eggplant is very tender, about 20 minutes.

Meanwhile, cook the pasta according to package directions.

Add spaghetti sauce to eggplant mixture, and simmer to heat through. Toss hot pasta with sauce.

Tips and Variations

Salting eggplant and letting it drain for $^1/_2$ hour or so eliminates some of the bitter flavor that the vegetable can have. In a pinch, however, this step can be skipped. Still, we always let the eggplant drain while preparing other parts of a recipe—even if it's just for a few minutes.

Spaghetti with "Meaty" Sauce

Makes 4 servings

Here is a way to add homemade taste to bottled sauce. Fresh mushrooms and textured vegetable protein make this a hearty sauce with a meaty texture. Serve it over your favorite pasta. We like angel hair because it cooks up in a flash.

2 tablespoons olive oil

$^1/_2$ to $^3/_4$ pound fresh mushrooms, sliced

1 cup textured vegetable protein

$^7/_8$ cup boiling water

One (32-ounce) jar meatless spaghetti sauce

One (15-ounce) can diced tomatoes, undrained

1 pound uncooked pasta

In a large, deep skillet, heat oil over medium heat. Add mushrooms, and simmer until tender, 7 to 8 minutes.

Meanwhile, in a small bowl, pour water over textured vegetable protein. Let stand 5 minutes; then add to mushrooms. Add spaghetti sauce and tomatoes, and simmer until heated through, 5 minutes. Cook pasta according to package directions. Drain pasta and top with sauce.

Pasta with Tapenade

Makes 4 servings

The most time-consuming thing about making your own tapenade (a paste or spread made with olives sometimes called kalamata olive spread) is pitting the olives. But you can purchase ready-made tapenade in most gourmet stores. It is somewhat pricey; but it's very heavy with flavor, and a little goes a long way. The tapenade is wonderful mixed with other ingredients and combined with fresh pasta.

1 pound fresh pasta

$^1/_2$ cup tapenade

2 roma tomatoes, diced

One (6$^1/_2$-ounce) jar marinated artichoke hearts, drained and chopped

$^1/_4$ cup chopped fresh basil (optional)

Zest of 1 lemon

2 to 4 tablespoons cup toasted pine nuts

2 tablespoons finely chopped fresh parsley

Cook pasta according to package directions. Drain, but don't rinse, and place in a large bowl. Add tapenade, tomatoes, artichokes, basil, if desired, and lemon zest; toss to combine all ingredients. Just before serving, toss with pine nuts and parsley.

Tips and Variations

If you have tapenade left over, you can make a delicious spread. In the bowl of a food processor fitted with the steel blade, blend $^1/_2$ cup tapenade with $^1/_2$ cup soft silken tofu, and process until smooth. Place in small bowl, and stir in $^1/_4$ cup minced fresh parsley.

This makes a lovely spread that is milder and smoother than tapenade and is wonderful on French bread. You can also toss the spread with cold pasta, chopped tomatoes, and 1 cup baby spinach to make a tasty pasta salad.

Pepper and Olive Pasta

Makes 4 servings

This dish, created by Linda Means of Michigan, has a wonderful gourmet quality to it but is tossed together with a minimum of fuss. A salad and warm Italian bread will round out the meal.

1 pound thin spaghetti or penne

4 scallions (green onions), thinly sliced

2 cloves garlic, minced

2 tablespoons olive oil

One (15-ounce) can garbanzo beans (chickpeas) or 2 cups cooked

2 large roasted red bell peppers (fresh roasted or canned), chopped

$2/3$ cup chopped black olives

$2/3$ cup chopped green olives

$1/2$ to 1 teaspoon cayenne pepper

$1/2$ cup toasted pine nuts (optional)

$1/2$ cup chopped oil-cured sun-dried tomatoes

Cook pasta according to package directions. Meanwhile, in a large saucepan, sauté scallions and garlic in oil over medium heat 3 minutes. Add garbanzo beans, roasted peppers, and olives. Stir in cayenne pepper. Simmer over low heat until flavors are blended, about 3 minutes.

Drain pasta, and toss with garbanzo bean mixture. Add pine nuts, if desired, and sun-dried tomatoes; toss to mix.

Hearty Soups and Stews

Soup Basics

Soup is a perfect way to use up little bits of leftovers. Using the ingredients that you love, you can create an endless variety of your own soup recipes. Here are some hints for making good soups and then some of our favorite recipes.

Thickeners for Soups and Stews

- For making hearty soups, stir in a cup of refried beans or black bean flakes.

- For more delicately flavored soups, add instant mashed potatoes for a smooth texture without altering the basic taste of the soup.

- Soups with a Mediterranean flavor can be thickened with French bread that has been quickly sautéed in olive oil. Add the bread, and then blend the soup with a handheld blender.

- To thicken a clear soup or sauce, whisk one teaspoon of cornstarch with two tablespoons of water, and stir into the hot soup. Continue stirring until it is thoroughly mixed, to avoid lumping.

Stock for Soups

- We love miso, a fermented paste of beans, as a starter for soup. Use $1/4$ cup miso for each $1 1/4$ cups of water—more or less to taste. Our favorite is white miso, a slightly sweet, caramel-colored miso with a pleasantly mild taste.

- Your own homemade vegetable stock will give soups a lovely, fresh flavor. Simmer onions, celery, and other vegetables in water for several hours, allowing the water to evaporate so that the stock cooks down somewhat. Strain, and use the broth as a starter for soup. This is a great way to use up bits and pieces of leftover vegetables. You can freeze the stock.

- There are many vegetable broth powders and bouillon cubes available. We've found a number of excellent ones in the bulk food section of our natural foods store and regular grocery store. Our favorite brand is Frontier, found in many bulk food sections. We keep a big jar on hand, because these are such a fast-and-easy way to add flavor to foods. Besides using these as a soup base, they are good for cooking rice and other grains.

Other Thoughts on Soups and Stews

- The flavor of soups and stews improves with age. Letting soup sit in the refrigerator for a day or so will allow the flavors to develop and intensify, so this is perfect make-ahead food. Make a big pot of soup on Sunday, and it will just get better throughout the week.

- Soup and stew seem to be such simple kinds of food that we think of them as casual supper dishes. But a good homemade soup is truly a gourmet delight. Served with a salad of baby greens, a warm loaf of French bread, and a glass of wine, any of our soups or stews makes perfect company fare. Your guests will never know that you were in and out of the kitchen in less than an hour!

Black Bean Soup with Orange Juice

Makes 6 servings

A winner in the Physicians Committee for Responsible Medicine recipe contest, this was contributed by David Beaupre. Its tangy, yet slightly sweet flavor definitely makes you want to ask for a second helping!

1 tablespoon olive oil

2 carrots finely diced

2 stalks celery, thinly sliced

1 medium onion, minced

1 cup vegetable broth

Two (15-ounce) cans black beans or 4 cups cooked

1/2 cup freshly squeezed orange juice

2 teaspoons ground cumin

2 teaspoons ground coriander

Juice of 2 limes

2 teaspoons salt

1 teaspoon freshly ground black pepper

In a large saucepan, heat oil over medium heat, and sauté carrots, celery, and onions until tender. Add broth, beans, orange juice, and spices; simmer, covered, 10 minutes. Add lime juice, salt, and pepper. With a hand blender, blend soup for about 30 seconds to thicken (or remove 1 cup of soup to a blender, purée and add back to soup pot).

Creamy Tomato Soup with Basil

Makes 4 servings

Soft tofu gives this soup its creamy quality. It is a beautiful starter for company dinner or a good main-dish soup with salad and bread. We also like it as a chilled soup. Serve it garnished with minced fresh basil and a sprinkling of freshly squeezed lime juice.

1 tablespoon olive oil

1 small onion, chopped

2 garlic cloves, minced

1^1/$_2$ cup vegetable broth

1 teaspoon dried basil

10 ounces soft or firm silken tofu

One (15-ounce) can diced tomatoes

One (15-ounce) can stewed tomatoes

Salt and freshly ground black pepper to taste

In a large saucepan, heat oil over medium heat, and sauté onions and garlic until tender. Add the remaining ingredients, and blend with an immersion blender until smooth.

Tips and Variations

If you don't have an immersion blender, you can purée the tofu and tomatoes in a food processor until smooth, and then stir together with the rest of the ingredients.

Tomato Lentil Soup

Makes 4 servings

This recipe was an entry to the Physicians Committee for Responsible Medicine recipe contest; and although not a prizewinner, it was a big hit with our testers. We would love to give credit to the contributor, but unfortunately, we couldn't read the name! It was too good to leave out of this book, and we thank our mystery contributor. You can use either red or brown lentils with this soup; it will cook a little more quickly with the red ones. Allspice gives it a distinctive flavor.

$1^1/_2$ cups water

$1/_2$ cup red lentils

3 stalks celery, sliced

2 carrots, sliced

$1/_2$ inch piece gingerroot, minced

1 small onion, coarsely chopped

3 ripe roma tomatoes, diced, or one (15-ounce) can diced

1 teaspoon salt

2 teaspoons cumin

1 teaspoon allspice

In a large pot, bring water to a boil. Add lentils, celery, carrots, ginger, and onion. Reduce heat, and simmer until lentils are tender, about 30 minutes. Add tomatoes and seasonings; simmer until heated through, about 5 minutes.

Spicy Pumpkin Soup

Makes 6 servings

This delicate and slightly sweet soup is good either hot or cold. You can alter the taste with the addition of $^1/_4$ to $^1/_2$ cup dry sherry or 1 tablespoon curry paste.

One (29-ounce) can pumpkin

4 cups plain soymilk

2 tablespoons margarine

1 tablespoon firmly packed brown sugar or Sucanat

$^1/_2$ cup freshly squeezed orange juice

1 tablespoon soy sauce

1 teaspoon dried tarragon

1 teaspoon chili powder

$^1/_4$ teaspoon cinnamon

$^1/_4$ teaspoon mace

In a large saucepan, combine pumpkin, soymilk, margarine and sugar; and heat slowly, stirring, over low heat. Add remaining ingredients, and cook over low heat until heated through, 2 to 3 minutes. Serve hot or cold.

Curried Cabbage and Corn Chowder

Makes 6 servings

This hearty soup, with a list of rather unusual ingredients, is a meal-in-one. Served with bread, it makes a quick-and-satisfying supper.

2 tablespoons olive oil

1 medium onion, chopped

3 carrots sliced $^1/_8$ inch thick

$^1/_2$ head cabbage, shredded

3 to 4 cups vegetable broth

1 cup tomato sauce

One (15-ounce) can vegetarian refried beans

One (15-ounce) can creamed corn

1 tablespoon soy sauce

1 to 2 teaspoons curry powder or 1 tablespoon paste

In a large saucepan, heat oil over medium heat, and sauté onion, carrots, and cabbage until cabbage is wilted and slightly tender. In a soup pot combine broth, tomato sauce, beans, corn, soy sauce, and curry powder. Add sautéed vegetables, and cook over low heat until heated through, about 10 minutes.

Refried Bean Soup with Chunky Chili Tomatoes

Makes 4 servings

You can replace canned refried beans with bean flakes in this easy-to-make hearty soup.

1 cup water or veggie broth

1 cup frozen corn kernels

1 cup chopped red or green bell peppers (optional)

$^1/_4$ cup chopped fresh cilantro (optional)

$^1/_2$ to 1 tablespoon chili powder or Mexican seasoning mix

$^1/_2$ teaspoon cumin

$^1/_2$ teaspoon garlic salt

One (30-ounce) or two (15-ounce) cans vegetarian refried beans

One (15.5-ounce) can chunky Mexican-style stewed tomatoes

Combine all ingredients in a large pot, and simmer gently over low heat until heated through, 5 minutes. Remove from heat, and let sit, covered, 5 to 8 minutes before serving.

Quick and Rich Veggie Stew

Makes 4 servings

Contributed by Julie Humiston of Minneapolis, this is a Physicians Committee for Responsible Medicine quick-fix contest winner. The tomatoes, sherry, and nutritional yeast produce a rich flavor for a very savory stew.

1 tablespoon olive oil

1 medium onion, coarsely chopped

3 cloves garlic, minced

1 cup water

1 large potato, diced

One (15-ounce) can diced carrots

One-half (10-ounce) bag fresh spinach

$1/2$ cup chopped parsley

2 tablespoons dry sherry

2 tablespoons nutritional yeast

2 teaspoons dried thyme

1 large carrot, thinly sliced

One (15-ounce) can garbanzo beans (chickpeas)

In a large pot, heat oil over medium heat, and sauté onion and garlic until onion is tender, 7 minutes. Add water, potato, and carrots. Bring to a boil; then lower heat, and simmer until vegetables are tender, about 10 minutes. Coarsely chop spinach, and add to pot. Add the remaining ingredients, and cook until spinach is wilted and stew is heated through, 3 minutes.

Mexican Stew with Chili Beans and Chipotle Peppers

Makes 4 servings

Chipotle peppers are smoked jalapeños, and they lend a wonderful musky, smoky flavor to recipes. S&W brand makes the chili beans with chipotle peppers that we've used in this recipe.

2$^1/_2$ cups vegetable broth

1 cup frozen corn

$^1/_2$ cup uncooked bulgur or 1 cup cooked brown rice

$^1/_4$ cup chopped fresh cilantro

1 tablespoon chili powder or Mexican seasoning mix

Dash of Tabasco or hot sauce to taste

1 avocado, sliced (optional)

One (15-ounce) can chili beans with chipotle peppers

One (15-ounce) can Mexican-style stewed tomatoes

In a large pot, mix all ingredients, except avocado, and simmer gently over low heat, 20 minutes. Remove from heat, and let sit, covered, 5 to 8 minutes to allow flavors to blend. Garnish with avocado, if desired, and serve.

Tips and Variations

If you don't have Mexican-style stewed tomatoes, use plain diced tomatoes and add an extra dash of Mexican seasoning. You can also substitute taco seasoning for Mexican seasoning in this recipe.

Portuguese Stew with Spinach and "Sausage"

Makes 4 servings

This hearty, tasty soup or stew is definitely a meal-in-one. It's great with crusty garlic bread.

2 cups vegetable broth

$1/2$ cup uncooked elbow macaroni

One (10-ounce) package frozen spinach

2 to 3 vegetarian "sausage" patties or links

One (15-ounce) can seasoned white beans

One (15.5-ounce) can diced tomatoes

1 to 2 teaspoons fennel seeds

1 teaspoon dried tarragon

Salt and freshly ground black pepper to taste

In a large pot, bring vegetable broth to a boil, and add the macaroni; cook until pasta is almost tender, 8 minutes. Add spinach, and cook until spinach is thawed, 10 minutes.

In another large pot, crumble the "sausage" patties into bite-sized pieces. Add beans, tomatoes, herbs, and salt and black pepper. Simmer briefly; then stir in the macaroni mixture.

Tips and Variations

Look for frozen vegetarian "sausage" patties in the breakfast area of the frozen foods section in your grocery store.

You can use chopped fresh spinach or kale in this recipe, too. If using kale, add it to the cooking water after the macaroni has cooked just 3 or 4 minutes, and allow the macaroni and kale to cook until the kale is tender, about 8 minutes.

Main-Dish Salads and Some Special Dressings

Salads are wonderful make-ahead meals. When you take the salad out of the refrigerator, be sure to let it sit for a few minutes to come to room temperature. Many Mediterranean foods are served this way, and the flavor of the vegetables is often better when they are not completely chilled or when they are allowed to sit for a few minutes at room temperature.

We also recommend blanching raw vegetables before adding them to salads. Some raw vegetables, such as celery and carrots, add a nice crunch to dishes. But blanching vegetables such as broccoli, green beans, and cauliflower improves their taste and brightens up their colors. Just drop them in a pot of boiling water and cook for about two minutes. Then drain and rinse immediately in cold running water. You can also steam the vegetables for one or two minutes.

Rainbow Dinner Salad

Makes 4 servings

Brightly colored vegetables give this main-dish salad, created by Julie Humiston of Minneapolis, an especially festive look. Serve it with a loaf of French bread for a filling meal that couldn't be easier.

1¹/₂ cups broccoli florets

One (10-ounce) bag mixed washed salad greens

One (15-ounce) can sliced or julienne beets, drained

One (15-ounce) can small white beans, drained

1 large carrot, peeled and thinly sliced

1 teaspoon dried basil

1 teaspoon dried thyme

Freshly ground black pepper to taste

2 tablespoons olive oil

2 tablespoons balsamic vinegar

2 tablespoons salted, roasted sunflower seeds

In a vegetable steamer, steam broccoli until slightly tender and bright green, 2 minutes. Place in refrigerator to cool.

In a large bowl, toss together salad greens, beets, beans, and carrot slices. Sprinkle on herbs and black pepper. In a small bowl, mix oil and vinegar; drizzle onto salad. Add broccoli, and toss lightly. Sprinkle sunflower seeds on top.

Mediterranean Black-Eyed Pea Salad

Makes 4 servings

This salad is so popular with our families that we usually double the recipe so we're sure to have some leftover for lunch the next day. The slightly earthy taste of the black-eyed peas is nicely offset by the lemon juice and olive oil.

One (10-ounce) package frozen chopped spinach

$1/2$ cucumber

1 medium tomato

One (15-ounce) can black-eyed peas or 2 cups cooked

2 teaspoons dried thyme

2 tablespoons olive oil

2 tablespoons freshly squeezed lemon juice

1 clove garlic minced

Salt and freshly ground black pepper to taste

Cook spinach according to package directions; drain well. Meanwhile, dice cucumber and tomato. In a medium saucepan, combine spinach, tomato, black-eyed peas, and thyme. Simmer until heated through, 5 minutes; remove from heat. Add cucumbers. In a small bowl, combine oil, lemon juice, and garlic, salt and pepper. Toss with black-eyed pea mixture. Serve warm or cold.

Tips and Variations

Nothing is more delicious than juicy, sweet fresh tomatoes, nor is any food quite so disappointing than the flavorless, pulpy, light pink vegetable that masquerades as a tomato. Shipped green to prevent damage, these tomatoes never ripen into edible produce.

If you want fresh tomatoes during the winter, the roma tomatoes are your best bet; often they can use several additional days of ripening when you bring them home from the store. Drained canned Italian tomatoes make another good substitute to use in sauces.

Lentil Rice Salad with Mustard Dressing

Makes 4 servings

This is a super way to use up leftover rice and lentils, or any combination of leftover grains and beans. The dressing offers an unusual combination of an Asian vinegar with the Mediterranean flavor of olive oil and lemon juice. We think the result is really special. Other vegetables that work nicely in this salad are peas, blanched green beans, and a few tablespoons of shredded jicama.

Salad

$1^1/_2$ cups broccoli florets

$1^1/_2$ cups cooked rice

2 cups cooked lentils
($^1/_2$ cup uncooked)

1 large tomato, chopped

$^1/_4$ cup currants

1 tablespoon snipped fresh parsley

1 stalk celery, diced

1 medium carrot, diced

1 small bunch (about 6) scallions (green onions), sliced, including green portion

Dressing

2 tablespoons seasoned rice vinegar

2 tablespoons olive oil

1 tablespoon freshly squeezed lemon juice

1 teaspoon Dijon mustard

Salt and freshly ground black pepper to taste.

In a large pot, blanch broccoli by dropping it into boiling water and cooking 2 minutes. Drain, and immediately rinse under cool running water. In a large bowl, combine all salad ingredients.

Make the dressing. In a jar with a tightly fitting lid, combine vinegar, oil, lemon juice and mustard; shake well. Pour over salad, and toss to mix. Season with salt and pepper to taste.

Tips and Variations

Leftovers make a great wrap. Add cubes of cooked potatoes to leftover salad, and mix with the dressing; then wrap in a whole wheat flour tortilla.

Moroccan Minted Couscous Salad

Makes 4 servings

Couscous flavored with mint and lemon juice is a part of traditional Mediterranean cuisine. This dish makes a good light supper in the summer and is lovely for picnics. Serve it at room temperature. For a more filling entrée, you might add 1 cup cooked white beans (baby limas, cannellinis, etc.) and adjust the flavorings a bit. This recipe calls for refined couscous, but you can use whole wheat if you prefer; just let it stand 10 to 15 minutes.

$3^1/2$ cups water

1 cup refined couscous

$3^1/2$ tablespoons olive oil

1 teaspoon salt or 1 vegetable bouillon cube

1 carrot, julienned

1 zucchini, julienned

$1/2$ cup raisins soaked in $3/4$ cup warm water

2 tablespoons chopped fresh mint or 2 teaspoons dried

$1/3$ to $1/2$ cup chopped fresh parsley or 2 tablespoons dried

3 tablespoons freshly squeezed lemon juice

Salt and freshly ground black pepper to taste

In a saucepan, bring $1^1/2$ cups of the water to a boil; add couscous, 1 tablespoon of the oil, and salt. Stir, return to a boil, and immediately remove from heat. Let sit, covered, until couscous is tender, 5 minutes. Fluff with a fork.

In another saucepan, bring remaining 2 cups water to a boil, and add carrot; boil 1 minute. Add zucchini; boil 2 minutes. Drain, and immediately rinse under cool running water. Drain again. Drain the raisins.

In a large bowl, combine couscous, raisins, vegetables, mint, and parsley. In a small bowl, whisk together lemon juice and remaining $2^1/2$ tablespoons oil; pour over couscous mixture. Toss gently, and season with salt and black pepper. Serve at room temperature or chilled.

Basmati Rice Salad with Thai Peanut Sauce

Makes 4 servings

Basmati is a particularly fragrant, delicately flavored rice. It is typically white, but you can often find brown basmati in natural foods stores. The unusual combination of the sesame dressing and Thai peanut sauce creates an exquisite taste for this salad. Be sure to serve this at room temperature.

2 cups water

$1/2$ teaspoon salt

1 cup uncooked basmati rice

2 tablespoons Sesame Dressing (page 90)

1 cup frozen small green peas

2 large carrots grated in food processor

2 tablespoons Thai peanut sauce

Chopped scallions (green onions) or fresh cilantro for garnish

2 tablespoons toasted sesame seeds (optional)

In a large pot, bring water and salt to a boil, and add rice. Return to boil, lower heat, and cover. Simmer, covered, until the water is absorbed, 15 to 20 minutes. (Or cook rice in a pressure cooker, according to the instructions on page 34.)

Meanwhile, make the Sesame Dressing.

When rice is done, immediately stir in peas, and toss briefly to thaw. Add carrots, peanut sauce, and dressing. Mix thoroughly, and garnish with scallions; serve with sesame seeds, if desired.

Tips and Variations

Thai peanut sauce can be purchased at many Asian grocery stores as well as in gourmet shops. You can find it dried and bottled. To speed up preparation time, you might substitute a commercial shiitake dressing for our homemade sesame dressing. Try Annie's brand, available in most natural foods stores.

Oriental Barley and Shiitake Salad

Makes 4 servings

We adapted this delicious recipe from one sent to us by Dorleen Tong of San Francisco. It can be made ahead of time, and served either cold or at room temperature. Shiitake mushrooms add an indescribably rich, almost musky flavor to the dish.

2 cups vegetable broth

1 cup uncooked pearl barley

$1/4$ cup Ginger Vinaigrette (page 88)

3 to 4 fresh shiitake mushrooms, thinly sliced

1 bunch (about 6) scallions (green onions), thinly sliced, including green portion

1 large stalk celery, finely chopped

$1/4$ large red bell pepper, coarsely chopped

$1/2$ to 1 teaspoon minced fresh gingerroot

Soy sauce or tamari to taste

In a large saucepan, bring broth to a boil, and add barley. Reduce heat to simmer, cook, covered until all water is absorbed, 20 minutes.

Meanwhile, make Ginger Vinaigrette.

Transfer barley to a large bowl, and add mushrooms, celery, bell pepper, and gingerroot. Add tamari and dressing, and mix well. Serve at room temperature.

Homemade Salad Dressings

We rarely buy bottled salad dressings. You can mix up your own in just a few minutes for much better flavor at a fraction of the price. Except for Tahini Dressing (page 91), which should be used in three to four days, these dressings keep for several weeks in the refrigerator. We nearly always keep jars of Ginger Vinaigrette (page 88) and Sesame Dressing (page 90) on hand, because they give a flavor boost to many of our favorite grain salads.

Be sure to use high-quality ingredients in the dressings, such as fresh gingerroot, dark roasted sesame oil, and extra-virgin olive oil. When you use the best ingredients, just small amounts of the dressings will impart exquisite flavor to your dishes.

Ginger Vinaigrette

Makes 1 cup

Although this recipe calls for rice or cider vinegar, you can give it a special flavor by using a fruit-flavored vinegar. We've used canola oil in this dressing, which has a mild flavor, to let the other flavors predominate.

¹/₄ cup rice or cider vinegar

¹/₂ cup canola oil

2 tablespoons soy sauce

1 teaspoon herbes de Provence

1 tablespoon minced gingerroot or pickled ginger

1 tablespoon orange juice concentrate

1 clove garlic, pressed or minced

Combine all ingredients in a jar with a tightly fitting lid. Shake well to mix.

Balsamic Vinaigrette with Mustard

Makes 1 cup

Use a good-quality Dijon mustard in this dressing.

$^1/_2$ cup olive oil

$^1/_4$ cup balsamic vinegar

1 rounded tablespoon old-style or country-style Dijon mustard

1 tablespoon chopped fresh tarragon or 1 teaspoon dried

$^1/_2$ teaspoon garlic salt

$^1/_2$ teaspoon sugar (optional)

Combine all ingredients in a jar with a tightly fitting lid. Shake well to mix.

Sesame Dressing

Makes 1 cup

Roasted sesame oil, even in small amounts, has a very intense flavor, so it is best to use a noncompeting, mild oil—such as canola—to go with it.

$^1/_2$ **cup canola oil**

$^1/_4$ **cup cider vinegar**

1 to 2 tablespoons dark roasted sesame oil

2 teaspoons toasted sesame seeds

2 teaspoons soy sauce

1 medium fresh shiitake mushroom, finely minced

Combine all ingredients in a jar with a tightly fitting lid. Shake well to mix.

Tahini Dressing

Makes 1 cup

You'll need to stir this dressing to combine the ingredients completely. This dressing has a shorter shelf life than others, so try to use it within three to four days. Be sure to keep it in the refrigerator.

$1/4$ **cup water**

Juice of 1 lemon

$1/2$ **cup toasted tahini**

2 tablespoons canola oil

1 tablespoon cider vinegar

1 teaspoon herbs of your choice (optional)

1 teaspoon soy sauce

1 clove garlic, minced or pressed

Stir the water and lemon juice into the tahini, a small amount at a time until it is the desired consistency. Add the rest of the ingredients and stir to mix well.

Mystery Dressing

Makes 1 cup

Wheat germ is the mystery ingredient that gives this intriguing dressing its slightly sweet taste and an interesting texture. It is too heavy for tossed green salads, but it's wonderful on grain and bean salads. It makes an excellent dip for fresh vegetables.

$^1/_2$ **cup toasted wheat germ**

$^3/_4$ **cup canola oil**

$^1/_2$ **cup freshly squeezed lemon or lime juice**

$^1/_4$ **cup soy sauce**

1 teaspoon dark roasted sesame oil

2 cloves garlic, coarsely chopped

Place the wheat germ in the container of a blender; purée until it forms a fine powder. Add the remaining ingredients, and blend until thoroughly mixed.

Vegetables and Side Dishes

Portobello Mushrooms Stuffed with Spinach and Herbal Pâté

Makes 4 servings

These stuffed mushrooms make an elegant but satisfying light supper with fresh large breadsticks and a tossed green salad. They also make a nice appetizer. This recipe won a prize in our quick-fix recipe contest and was contributed by Doris Krauch of Lauderdale Lakes, Florida.

4 to 6 portobello mushroom caps

1 tablespoon olive oil

Salt to taste

One (10-ounce) package frozen chopped spinach, thawed

One (4¹/₂-ounce) can vegetarian pâté*

¹/₂ cup fresh bread crumbs

Freshly ground black pepper to taste

¹/₂ teaspoon mixed herbs

¹/₂ cup sliced almonds

Preheat the broiler. Rinse mushroom caps, and pat dry with a paper towel. Remove, and finely chop any stems. Brush caps lightly with oil and sprinkle very lightly with salt. Place caps, stem side down, and chopped stems on a cookie sheet; broil 6 inches from the element until tender and browned, about 6 minutes. Turn caps over, and stir the stems; broil until browned, 3 minutes.

Meanwhile, squeeze excess liquid from spinach. In a medium bowl, mix spinach, pâté, bread crumbs, pepper, herbs, and almonds. Add the mushroom stems. Spread spinach mixture into mushroom caps. Return to the broiler, and broil until golden, 4 to 5 minutes.

We like three different types of Bonavita: Vegetarian Herbal, Garlic, or Mushroom Pâté.

Lemon Portobello Mushrooms

Makes 4 servings

Serve these simple marinated mushrooms sandwich-style on rolls or add them to a grain salad. In the summer, use the marinade on whole portobello mushroom caps, and cook outdoors on the grill.

1 pound fresh portobello mushrooms, sliced

$^1/_4$ cup olive oil

1 tablespoon freshly squeezed lemon juice

$1^1/_2$ teaspoons freshly grated lemon zest

$^3/_4$ teaspoons Dijon mustard

$^1/_2$ teaspoon finely minced garlic

1 teaspoon finely minced fresh rosemary

Salt and freshly ground black pepper to taste

Preheat the broiler. Place the mushrooms in a single layer on a jellyroll pan. In a small bowl, whisk together the remaining ingredients, and pour over the mushrooms. Broil until tender and brown, 6 minutes.

Choucroute Sauerkraut with "Sausage"

Makes 3 to 4 servings

When Kate and her family were living in France, this was one of their favorite dishes, which they would buy at local charcouteries (delicatessen-like shops). The sautéed onions and vegetarian "sausage" make the sauerkraut both smooth and mild. It takes just minutes to prepare.

1 to 2 tablespoons olive oil

1 medium to large onion, chopped

3 vegetarian "sausage" patties

One (15-ounce) can sauerkraut, drained

1 teaspoon caraway or fennel seeds

In a large saucepan, heat oil over medium heat, and sauté onion until tender, about 8 minutes. Crumble "sausage" patties into bite-sized pieces, and add to onion. Sauté 1 minute. Add sauerkraut and caraway seeds; cook over low heat until just warm.

Coleslaw Made Easy

Makes 4 servings

The dash of five-spice powder and the ginger dressing make this rather traditional coleslaw especially tasty.

2 tablespoons Ginger Vinaigrette (page 88)

2 medium to large carrots

1 small or 1/2 large head cabbage

1/4 cup raisins

1/2 teaspoon five-spice powder

Make Ginger Vinaigrette. Grate carrots in a food processor or Mouli hand grater; transfer to a large bowl. Shred cabbage, and mix with carrots, and add raisins and five-spice powder. Pour on dressing, and toss.

Tips and Variations

If you don't have time to make the Ginger Vinaigrette, try a commercial dressing; we like White Swan brand Jaipur salad dressing.

Two Super-Easy Ways to Make Potatoes

Potatoes are so often relegated to the side. But we think either of these potato dishes makes a perfect entrée when served with steamed vegetables, a salad, and bread.

Golden Yukon Potatoes

Makes 4 servings

Yellow potatoes have a particularly creamy texture, and the unusual combination of olive oil and soy sauce imparts a wonderful flavor to them. This recipe is so simple it can hardly be called a recipe, but it is delicious!

4 to 6 medium yellow potatoes, such as Yukon Gold

1 tablespoon olive oil

1 tablespoon soy sauce

2 tablespoons finely chopped fresh parsley

Wash potatoes, but don't peel them; cut into walnut-sized chunks. In a large saucepan, cover potatoes with water; boil until just tender, 12 to 15 minutes. (Don't cook too long or potatoes will fall apart.) Drain, and toss with oil, soy sauce, and parsley.

Lemony Roasted Potatoes

Makes 4 servings

4 to 6 medium white, thin-skinned potatoes

1 tablespoon extra-virgin olive oil

1 medium onion, finely chopped

1 tablespoon freshly squeezed lemon juice

1 tablespoon snipped fresh rosemary

Salt to taste

Preheat oven to 400°F.

Cut potatoes into walnut-sized pieces, and place in a large bowl. In a frying pan, heat oil over medium heat, and sauté onion, 3 minutes. Spoon onion over potatoes. Drizzle lemon juice on top, and sprinkle with rosemary and salt. Toss to combine.

Spread in a single layer in a shallow baking pan, cover with aluminum foil, and bake 20 minutes. Remove foil, and bake 15 minutes, or until potatoes are tender.

Blanched Vegetables with Vinaigrette

Makes 4 servings

This is an easy and colorful way to fix marinated vegetables. The combination of vegetables is up to you; try choosing ones that take about the same time to cook.

6 cups water

2 cups broccoli florets and peeled stems cut in $^1/_2$-inch slices

2 cups cauliflower florets

2 carrots cut into $^1/_2$ inch slices

$^1/_4$ cup Balsamic Vinaigrette with Mustard (page 89)

1 small Vidalia or red onion, thinly sliced (optional)

Bring water to boil in a large pot. Put broccoli, cauliflower, and carrots in a large strainer, and submerge in the water. Cook until vegetables are tender-crisp and broccoli is bright green, 2 to 3 minutes. Remove from water, and drain well. Transfer to a large bowl. While vegetables are still hot, add Balsamic Vinaigrette with Mustard and onion. Toss to mix, add more vinaigrette, if desired, and serve at room temperature.

Garbanzo Bean and Tomato Salad

Makes 4 servings

Healthy, fast, and tasty too, this salad makes an easy side dish. Feel free to add other ingredients to it, such as sliced black olives, blanched green beans, thawed green peas, or whatever suits your fancy.

$^1/_4$ cup chopped fresh cilantro or parsley

1 small Vidalia or red onion, thinly sliced

1 clove garlic, finely chopped (optional)

One (15-ounce) can garbanzo beans (chickpeas), drained

One (15-ounce) can Mexican-style stewed tomatoes

In a large bowl, mix all ingredients. Serve at room temperature.

Tips and Variations

Vidalia onions are sweet and are especially wonderful in dishes that call for raw onions. Unfortunately, they are available only for a month or so in the spring. If you can't find them, substitute Texas sweet or red onions.

Jicama

Jicama is a delightful root vegetable that is very low in calories. It has a pleasant mild but slightly sweet taste, and a refreshingly crisp texture. It is great raw or cooked, and we often use it as a substitute for water chestnuts in Asian food. Sometimes when we are following a recipe that calls for jicama, we end up with more than we need and are left wondering how to use up the remaining amount. Here are a couple quick-and-easy recipes that make the most of jicama.

Jicama Salad with Mint and Oranges

Makes 4 servings

This easy salad is a wonderful, refreshing dish that travels well—perfect for pot lucks and picnics.

1 navel orange

1/4 cup chopped fresh mint or 1 tablespoon dried

2 cups julienned peeled jicama

1 small head Boston or Bibb lettuce, torn into pieces, or 4 cups baby spinach

1/2 avocado, sliced (optional)

Peel orange, divide in half, and cut in 1/4-inch-thick slices. In a medium bowl, mix orange, mint, and jicama; marinate several hours in the refrigerator. Serve on a bed of lettuce, and garnish with a few slices of avocado, if desired.

Sautéed Jicama and Mushrooms

Makes 2 servings

1 to 2 tablespoons olive oil

$^1/_2$ medium jicama, peeled
and sliced into 2-inch strips
($1^1/_2$ to 2 cups)

$1^1/_2$ cups sliced mushrooms

1 clove garlic, minced

1 to 2 teaspoons dried
tarragon

$^1/_2$ pound cooked spinach
noodles

1 teaspoon garlic-infused
olive oil

In a large saucepan, heat olive oil over medium heat, and sauté jicama and mushrooms until softened, 5 minutes. Add garlic and tarragon, and toss. Sauté 2 minutes. In a large bowl, toss noodles with garlic-infused oil; top with vegetable mixture.

Tips and Variations

Add $^1/_2$ cup cubed tofu and sauté with jicama and mushrooms to stretch the recipe.

To serve jicama as an appetizer, peel, cut in half, and slice fairly thinly (about $^1/_8$ inch thick). Spread these jicama "crackers" with homemade Salsa Verde (page 106) or Red Pepper Tofu Spread (page 112) or sprinkle with Mexican seasoning.

Pestos, Salsas, Sauces and Spreads

Pesto

Pesto seems so special that people rarely think of it as a quick meal. But these pestos are fast and easy. One recipe goes a long way—just a few tablespoons of pesto is enough for one serving of pasta—and it is also versatile and freezes well. Freeze any of these recipes in an ice cube tray for individual portions. Then pop them out and store in a zipper-locking bag in the freezer. Add a cube of pesto to soups, stews, or sauces for a savory flavor boost. Some other ideas for pesto:

- Turn a baked potato into a gourmet meal with a dollop or two of pesto.

- Spread bread with a thin layer of pesto and then make a sandwich of sliced raw or grilled vegetables.

- Give homemade or frozen pizzas some extra personality with a few spoonfuls of pesto.

- Use as a sauce for grilled tofu or vegetables.

- Spread crackers or slices of bread with pesto for a fast party appetizer.

- And, of course, the traditional way to serve pesto is tossed with pasta for a fast and festive dinner.

Sun-Dried Tomato Pesto

Makes about 2 cups

This keeps for ages in the refrigerator.

¹/₂ cup drained oil-cured sun-dried tomatoes

¹/₄ cup packed fresh basil leaves or 2 teaspoons dried

¹/₄ cup olive oil

2 to 3 tablespoons toasted pine nuts

2 large garlic cloves, coarsely chopped

¹/₄ to ¹/₂ cup finely chopped red bell pepper (optional)

Place all ingredients, except bell pepper, in the bowl of a food processor fitted with the steel blade, and process until well blended. Mix in bell pepper, if desired. Put in a small container, and refrigerate.

Oven-Dried Tomatoes

Makes about 4 cups

These tomatoes require little hands-on preparation but cook slowly for several hours. They will keep refrigerated for 2 to 3 weeks. Add them to pasta dishes, salads, soups, or spreads.

20 roma tomatoes, cut in half lengthwise

2 tablespoons olive oil

2 tablespoons balsamic vinegar

1 to 2 teaspoons dried Italian herb mix

1 to 2 teaspoons sugar, depending on the sweetness of the tomatoes

Preheat oven to 250°F. Place halved tomatoes on a cookie sheet, cut side up. Sprinkle with remaining ingredients. Bake until tomatoes are slightly shriveled but still retain some juiciness, about 6 hours.

Cilantro and Sesame Pesto

Makes about 1¹/₂ cups

Here is a delicious alternative to the more typical basil pesto. It's wonderful over pasta, rice, or baked potato.

1-inch piece gingerroot

1 to 2 cloves garlic

3 tablespoons toasted sesame seeds

1 cup cilantro, cleaned and stems removed

1 tablespoon soy sauce

1 tablespoon cider or raspberry vinegar

Juice of 1 lime or lemon

Dash of cayenne pepper

1 tablespoon dark roasted sesame oil

2 tablespoons canola oil

In the bowl of a food processor fitted with the steel blade, chop ginger and garlic. Add remaining ingredients except oils, and pulse until finely chopped. With the machine running, add oil in small amounts, and process until smooth. Keep, covered, in refrigerator for up to 2 weeks.

Salsa Verde

Serve this salsa at room temperature as an accompaniment to bean dishes, tacos, enchiladas, or any southwestern meal. This salsa freezes well.

2 cups chopped tomatillos

¹/₄ to ¹/₂ cup fresh cilantro, packed, whole leaves

1 to 2 tablespoons chopped jalapeño peppers*

¹/₂ teaspoon ground cumin

¹/₂ teaspoon whole cumin seeds

2 cloves garlic

1 small onion

Juice of ¹/₂ lime or lemon

Dash of salt

In a medium saucepan, simmer tomatillos in enough water to cover over low heat until not quite soft, about 6 minutes. In the bowl of a food processor fitted with the steel blade, combine remaining ingredients; process until fairly smooth. Add drained tomatillos, and process until mixture is a chunky purée.

Fresh chiles are great, but canned are quicker to use.

Tips and Variations

To enliven the flavor of any bottled salsa, add chopped cilantro and chopped scallions or sweet onions for a homemade taste.

Tomatillos can be found year-round in the produce section of most markets. They look like small green tomatoes wrapped in a papery husk; they have a tart, interesting taste somewhat like a green tomato. They are generally cooked and used in Mexican cuisine for salsa verde. Choose tomatillos that are firm with close-fitting husks with no black or mildewy spots. They will keep an amazingly long time in a paper bag in the fridge. To cook, peel off the husks, and rinse to remove the sticky substance near the stem.

White Bean and Celery Salsa

Makes about 4^1/$_2$ cups

One (15-ounce) can white beans (navy or cannellini), drained and rinsed

^{3}/$_4$ cup medium salsa

^{1}/$_4$ cup chopped fresh cilantro

1 teaspoon ground cumin

^{1}/$_4$ teaspoon cumin seeds

^{1}/$_4$ teaspoon salt

^{1}/$_4$ to ^{1}/$_2$ cup chopped red or Vidalia onions

2 stalks celery, thinly sliced

1 medium red bell pepper, finely chopped

In the bowl of a food processor fitted with the steel blade, process beans until smooth. Transfer to a medium bowl, add salsa, cilantro, cumin, cumin seeds, and salt; mix well. Add celery and bell pepper, and stir to combine. Refrigerate at least 4 hours before serving.

Enliven a platter of leftovers with a good, rich, flavorful sauce. Use any of our sauces over any combination of whatever happens to be in your refrigerator. They are perfect for leftover pasta, grains, steamed vegetables, and chunks of sautéed tofu or tempeh.

Lemon Tahini Sauce

Makes 1 cup

This is a traditional Mid-Eastern sauce. Serve it over grains tossed with vegetables and raisins or drizzle over a pita pocket stuffed with grilled vegetables.

$^1/_4$ **cup of water**

Juice of 1 lemon

$^1/_2$ **cup toasted tahini**

1 teaspoon soy sauce

1 clove garlic, minced or pressed, or 1 teaspoon garlic salt

1 teaspoon herbs of your choice (optional)

1 teaspoon country-style mustard (optional)

In a medium bowl, stir water and lemon juice into tahini a little bit at a time until well blended. Add soy sauce and garlic; mix well. Add herbs and mustard, if desired, stir to combine.

Orange Tahini Sauce

Makes 2¹/₂ cups

This sauce has a slightly sweet flavor that makes it a good choice to serve over spicy grain and bean dishes.

3 tablespoons canola oil

$^1/_2$ cup finely chopped onion

1 clove garlic, minced

1 cup tahini

$^1/_2$ cup freshly squeezed orange juice

Water

1 tablespoon tamari

1 teaspoon firmly packed brown sugar

$^1/_2$ teaspoon salt

In a saucepan, heat oil over medium heat, and sauté onion and garlic until the onion is tender, about 8 minutes. Stir in tahini, reduce heat to very low, and cook, stirring constantly, 5 minutes. Stir in orange juice and enough water to produce desired consistency. Add the remaining ingredients, increase the heat to a simmer, and cook until heated through, 5 minutes.

Indonesian Peanut Sauce

Makes 4 cups

Spicy peanut sauce is traditional in the cuisine of Indonesia. We love this over almost any combination of leftover grains, beans, potatoes, tofu, and vegetables.

2 tablespoons canola oil

1 medium onion, coarsely chopped

2 cloves garlic, minced

2 teaspoons minced gingerroot

1 cup smooth peanut butter

2 cups water

1 tablespoon firmly packed brown sugar

1 tablespoon freshly squeezed lemon juice

1 tablespoon cider vinegar

1 teaspoon salt

$1/4$ teaspoon cayenne pepper

In a large saucepan, heat oil over medium heat, and sauté the onion, garlic, and gingerroot until onions are tender, about 8 minutes. Add peanut butter and water; stir until completely combined. Add the remaining ingredients. Simmer over very low heat until thick and bubbly, 20 minutes. Add more water if sauce gets too thick and bubbly.

Mushroom and Miso Sauce

Makes 2¹/₂ cups

Miso gives a rich, full-bodied taste to this sauce. Choose a mellow, light miso so the mushrooms will not be overpowered. This is especially good served over a baked potato.

2 teaspoons olive oil

¹/₂ cup finely chopped onion

4 cups sliced mushrooms

³/₄ cup vegetable broth

2 to 3 tablespoons miso, thinned with ³/₄ cup hot water

1 tablespoon flour mixed with ¹/₄ cup water (optional)

In a large saucepan, heat oil over medium heat, and sauté onion, 1 to 2 minutes. Add mushrooms; cook until they are limp, 2 minutes. Add broth and miso, cover, and simmer gently until thickened, about 10 minutes. For a thicker sauce, purée half the mixture in a blender or processor; then return to the pan. Or slowly add the flour mixture to the sauce. Simmer gently until thickened.

Spreads

Spreads are a great way to fill out a meal. Easy to prepare and wonderfully versatile, they act as a dip with vegetables for a quick snack, or provide the basis for a hearty sandwich.

Red Pepper Tofu Spread

Makes 4 servings

This spread is great for a sandwich filling or as a dip for raw vegetables.

1 cup soft tofu or soft silken

$1/3$ cup cashews

$1/4$ cup chopped sweet onions (Texas, Vidalia, or red)

$1/4$ cup oil-cured sun-dried tomatoes

1 tablespoon mild miso or soy sauce

1 tablespoon Dijon mustard

$1/2$ large red bell pepper, coarsely chopped

Put all ingredients in blender, and purée just until smooth.

Tips and Variations

If you don't have tofu on hand, substitute one (15-ounce) can of small white beans, drained. It makes a slightly firmer spread. You can also add some beans to the tofu spread if it seems too runny.

Black and Butter Bean Spread with Oven-Dried Tomatoes

Makes about 4 cups

This is a tasty dip to serve with toasted pita triangles or as a spread for French bread or a sandwich filling.

$^1/_4$ **cup coarsely cut Oven-Dried Tomatoes (recipe follows) or oil-cured sun-dried**

$^1/_4$ **cup fresh cilantro, packed, whole leaves**

$^1/_8$ **cup water**

2 tablespoons freshly squeezed lemon juice

1 tablespoon olive oil

1 clove garlic

One (15-ounce) can butter beans, drained

One (15-ounce) can black beans, drained

Make the Oven-Dried Tomatoes. In the bowl of a food processor fitted with the steel blade, blend all ingredients until smooth.

Our Favorite Hummus Recipes

We love most beans, but garbanzo beans are among our favorites. They have a delicious taste and texture all by themselves, are wonderful puréed or mixed with a variety of ingredients, and are neither overpowering nor overpowered by other flavors. Garbanzo beans are a staple in Mid-Eastern cookery, especially for making hummus. Traditional hummus combines garbanzo beans, sesame tahini, and lemon juice for a smooth spread that is wonderful stuffed into a pita bread pocket and topped with chopped tomatoes and cucumbers. Here we've offered our favorite recipe for that spread as well as two not-so-traditional but equally wonderful hummus variations. A platter of raw vegetables and pita wedges with a bowl of hummus makes for a fun and filling meal.

Traditional Hummus

Makes 2¹/₂ cups

¹/₄ cup packed fresh parsley

¹/₂ cup tahini

¹/₄ cup freshly squeezed lemon juice

1 to 2 cloves garlic

Salt to taste

One (15-ounce) can garbanzo beans (chickpeas), drained (about ¹/₂ cups)

In the bowl of a food processor fitted with the steel blade, process the parsley until well chopped. Add remaining ingredients, and process until smooth.

Hummus with Cilantro

Makes 2¹/₂ cups

¹/₄ cup packed fresh cilantro or basil

¹/₄ cup freshly squeezed lemon juice

¹/₄ cup olive oil

1 teaspoon garlic salt

One (15-ounce) can garbanzo beans (chickpeas) beans, drained (about 1¹/₂ cups)

In the bowl of a food processor fitted with the steel blade, chop cilantro. Add remaining ingredients and process until smooth.

Tips and Variations

Add 1 teaspoon Patak brand curry paste to give this recipe a whole new spicy taste.

Hummus with Sun-Dried Tomatoes

Makes 2¹/₂ cups

¹/₄ cup oil-cured sun-dried tomatoes

¹/₄ cup freshly squeezed lemon juice

2 to 4 tablespoons oil from oil-cured sun-dried tomatoes

1 teaspoon garlic salt

One (15-ounce) can garbanzo beans (chickpeas) beans, drained (about 1¹/₂ cups)

In the bowl of a food processor fitted with the steel blade, chop sun-dried tomatoes. Add remaining ingredients, and to desired consistency.

Mock Tuna Spread

Makes about 5$^1/_2$ cups

This chunky spread reminds us of tuna salad and is great stuffed into a pita pocket or served as a party spread with crackers. Its tunalike flavor comes from the addition of kelp powder.

Two (15-ounce) cans garbanzo beans (chickpeas), well drained, or 4 cups cooked, well drained

$^1/_2$ cup eggless mayonnaise

2 tablespoons freshly squeezed lemon juice

1 tablespoon kelp powder

1 stalk celery, coarsely chopped

1 small onion, finely chopped

Salt and freshly ground black pepper to taste

In the bowl of a food processor fitted with the steel blade, process garbanzo beans until coarsely chopped, just a few seconds. Transfer to a medium bowl, and add the remaining ingredients. Mix well. Adjust seasonings with salt, pepper, and lemon juice, if desired.

5

Quick Mixes: Creating Your Own Convenience Foods

Quick mixes for baking have a long history in the kitchens of busy and efficient cooks. We've created some ideas especially for vegetarian cooks. For example, you can stock your shelf with mixes for rice pilaf, chili, tacos, and sloppy Joes. If commercial rice dishes contain too many additives for your taste or, you don't like the idea of using polished rice, you can make up your own mix, using brown rice, vegetable broth, and seasonings. Keep a big jar of it on hand, and you can make terrific rice pilaf at a fraction of the price of the store-bought kind, but without finding and measuring six or seven different ingredients every time you cook.

Making your own mixes for these dishes takes just fifteen minutes or so. Prepare them in large quantities and store on the shelf or in the refrigerator, and they will save you time over and over again when you use them for a variety of dinners. For example, our simple Chili Mix allows you to make Three Bean Chili and Old-Fashioned Meatless Chili in just minutes. In fact, with just three or four basic recipes in stock, you can create as many as fifteen different entrées in minutes. In some cases, a mix is used for just one recipe, but because these recipes are among our favorites, we use them over and over again; so it is worthwhile to have the mix on hand.

The addition of vegetable broth powder causes some of these mixes to pack down rather firmly. Before using, stir them with a wooden spoon; and with the lid securely closed, give the jar a couple of good shakes to loosen mix.

Onion-Flavored Rice Mix

Makes about 5 cups

4 cups uncooked white or brown rice

1/2 cup vegetable broth powder

1/2 cup dried onion flakes

1/4 cup dried parsley

1 teaspoon salt

In a jar with a tightly fitting lid, mix all ingredients.

Basic Onion-Flavored Rice

Makes 4 servings

2 cups water

1 tablespoon margarine

1 cup Onion-Flavored Rice Mix (above)

In a medium saucepan, combine water and margarine; bring to a boil. Add Onion-Flavored Rice Mix, and return to a simmer. Cook, covered, over medium-low heat until all water is absorbed, about 20 minutes for white rice or 40 minutes for brown.

Onion-Flavored Rice with Sautéed Mushrooms and Garlic

Makes 4 servings

1 tablespoon olive oil

1¹/₂ to 2 cups sliced mushrooms (about 16 medium)

1 clove garlic minced

3 cups cooked Basic Onion-Flavored Rice (page 119)

1 teaspoon garlic-infused olive oil (optional)

In a large saucepan, heat oil over medium heat, and sauté mushrooms until just slightly brown, 4 minutes. Add garlic, and sauté briefly. Stir in the Basic Onion-Flavored Rice, and add garlic-infused oil for a rich flavoring, if desired.

Vegetable Rice Mix

Makes about 4 cups

Look for dehydrated vegetable mixes in the bulk food section of grocery stores or natural foods markets. It is often labeled as a *soup mix* or *starter*. They tend to be very expensive by weight, but ¹/₂ cup of this mix weighs little more than 1 ounce. For a mix with a slightly nuttier flavor, try mixing half white rice with half bulgur.

4 cups uncooked white or brown rice

¹/₂ cup dehydrated vegetables

¹/₄ cup vegetable broth powder

2 teaspoons salt

In a jar with a tightly fitting lid, mix all ingredients.

Basic Vegetable Rice

Makes 4 servings

2 cups water

1 tablespoon margarine

1 cup Vegetable Rice Mix
(page 120)

In a medium saucepan, combine water and margarine; bring to a boil. Add Vegetable Rice Mix, and return to simmer. Cook, covered, over medium heat until all water is absorbed, about 20 minutes for white rice and 40 minutes for brown.

Vegetable Rice with White Beans and Corn

Makes 4 servings

3 cups water

1 cup broccoli florets

1 carrot sliced $1/4$-inch thick

3 cups cooked Basic Vegetable Rice (above)

1 cup cooked (or $2/3$ can) white beans (navy beans, cannellini)

$1/2$ cup frozen corn kernels, thawed

$1/2$ cup frozen peas, thawed

$1/2$ cup Ginger (page 88) or Balsamic Vinaigrette (page 89) salad dressing

In a medium saucepan, bring water to a boil. Add broccoli and carrot; boil until blanched, 2 minutes. Remove from heat, drain, and set aside. In a large bowl, mix Basic Vegetable Rice, beans, corn, and peas. Add broccoli and carrots. Mix in enough dressing to moisten. Serve at room temperature.

Vegetable Rice with Savory Baked Tofu and Mushrooms

Makes 4 servings

1 tablespoon olive oil

8 ounces sliced mushrooms

8 ounces baked tofu, diced

3 cups cooked Basic Vegetable Rice (page 121)

In a large saucepan, heat oil over medium heat, and sauté mushrooms until tender, 6 minutes. Add tofu, and sauté until tofu is heated through, 5 minutes. Add Vegetable Rice, and toss to combine.

Tips and Variations

You can buy baked tofu in the produce section of most grocery stores or you can make your own: Dice 8 ounces tofu and spread out on a baking sheet.

Mix 2 tablespoons soy sauce, $1/2$ tablespoon pure maple syrup, and 1 tablespoon water. Pour over tofu. Bake at 350°F 30 minutes. Or try the Baked Five-Spice Tofu on page 49.

Lemon-Dill Rice Pilaf

Makes 4 servings

2 cups cold water

1 cup Lemon-Dill Rice Mix
(below)

1 tablespoon olive oil

In a large saucepan, bring water to a
boil. Add Lemon-Dill Rice Mix and
olive oil; return to a boil. Reduce heat,
and simmer, covered until all water is
absorbed, about 40 minutes.

Lemon-Dill Rice Mix

Makes 8 cups

8 cups uncooked brown rice

5 tablespoons vegetable
broth powder

3 tablespoons dried grated
lemon peel

3 tablespoons dried dill

4 teaspoons dried minced
chives

In large bowl, mix all ingredients.

Lemon-Dill Rice Salad

Makes 4 servings

3 cups cooked Lemon-Dill Rice Pilaf (page 123)

1 to 2 carrots, halved lengthwise and sliced $1/8$ inch thick

$1/2$ cup frozen baby peas (petit pois), thawed

$1/2$ to 1 cup broccoli florets, blanched

Vinaigrette dressing to taste

Let Lemon-Dill Rice Pilaf cool. Transfer to a large bowl, and add carrots, peas, and broccoli. Toss with vinaigrette.

Lemon-Dill Rice with Garbanzo Beans and Sun-Dried Tomatoes

Makes 4 servings

3 cups hot cooked Lemon-Dill Rice Pilaf (page 123)

One (15-ounce) can garbanzo beans (chickpeas), drained (about 1^1/$_2$ cups)

^{1}/$_4$ cup chopped oil-cured sun-dried tomatoes

2 tablespoons chopped fresh parsley or 1 tablespoon dried

1 tablespoon chopped fresh mint or 1 teaspoon dried

Juice of ^{1}/$_2$ lemon

^{1}/$_4$ cup toasted sunflower seeds

While Lemon-Dill Rice Pilaf is still hot, stir in garbanzo beans, tomatoes, and herbs. Right before serving, add lemon juice; fluff with a fork, and garnish with sunflower seeds.

Lentil and Rice Mix

Makes 1 cup

This is the mix that Kate used when living on her boat. To make sure that each recipe has the right proportion of carrots, rice, and lentils, you can do as she did: Make up individual packets in small zipper-locking bags; then store bags in a plastic air-tight container. This recipe gives the proportions for 1 packet.

$3/4$ **cup uncooked white rice**

$1/4$ **cup uncooked lentils**

$1/4$ **cup dried carrots or dried vegetable mix**

2 tablespoons dried onion flakes

1 tablespoon vegetable broth powder or vegetable bouillon cube

1 tablespoon dried parsley flakes

1 teaspoon of mixed herbs

In zipper-locking plastic bag, mix all ingredients.

Basic Lentil and Rice

Makes 4 servings

2^1/$_4$ cups water

1 packet (1 cup) Lentil and Rice Mix (page 126)

1 tablespoon oil

In a medium saucepan, bring water to a boil. Add Lentil Rice Mix and oil; stir briefly. Reduce heat, and simmer, covered, 20 minutes. Remove from heat, and let sit covered 5 minutes; fluff with a fork before serving.

Orzo with Chicken-Flavored Vegetable Broth and Onion Mix

Makes 4 cups

Orzo, or small rice-shaped pasta, is usually cooked like other pasta—in a large amount of water and then drained. We have found that it cooks quite nicely when cooked like white rice. For that reason, it works very well in a mix.

4 cups orzo

1/2 cup chicken-flavored vegetable broth powder

5 teaspoons dried onion flakes

5 teaspoons dried parsley

In a jar with a tightly fitting lid, mix all ingredients.

Basic Orzo Pilaf

Makes 4 servings

2 cups water

1 cup Orzo with Chicken-Flavored Vegetable Broth and Onion Mix (page 128)

1/4 teaspoon garlic-infused olive oil (optional)

In a medium saucepan, bring water to a boil. Add Orzo with Chicken-Flavored Broth and Onion Mix; return to a boil. Lower heat, and cook, covered, until all water is absorbed, 15 minutes. Toss with garlic-infused olive oil, if desired, before serving.

Orzo with Mushrooms

Makes 4 servings

2 tablespoons olive oil

¹/₂ pound mushrooms, sliced

3 cups cooked Basic Orzo Pilaf (page 129)

In a large saucepan, heat oil over medium heat, and sauté mushrooms until tender. Add Basic Orzo Pilaf, and toss to mix thoroughly.

Cream of Potato Soup Mix

Makes 9 cups

Cream of potato soup makes a hearty winter meal. With our mix, you can have soup on the table in about 5 minutes. This mix makes a thick soup; if you like yours a little thinner, add extra vegetable broth.

8 cups dried potato flakes

1¹/₂ cups chicken-flavored vegetable broth powder

1 cup soymilk powder

¹/₂ cup dried onion flakes

¹/₄ cup dried chives

¹/₄ cup dried parsley

In a jar with a tightly fitting lid, mix all ingredients.

Cream of Potato Soup

Makes 6 servings

Serve this soup either hot or chilled. If serving it chilled, you will need to add a bit of extra vegetable broth or soy milk to thin it; garnish it with fresh snipped chives.

6 cups water

2^1/$_2$ cups Cream of Potato Soup Mix (page 131)

Freshly squeezed lemon juice (optional)

In a large pot, bring the water to a boil. Remove from heat, and while stirring, add Cream of Potato Soup Mix. Return to very low heat, and cook just to heat through, 3 to 4 minutes. Sprinkle with fresh lemon juice, if desired.

Corn Chowder

Makes 4 servings

3 cups water

1¹/₄ cups Cream of Potato Soup Mix (page 131)

1 cup frozen or canned corn, drained

1 cup cooked cubed potatoes

One (15-ounce) can cream-style corn

Salt and freshly ground black pepper to taste (optional)

In a soup pot, combine all ingredients. Cook over very low heat just to heat through, 3 to 4 minutes.

Curried Potato Soup

Makes 4 servings

3 cups water

1¹/₄ cups Cream of Potato Soup Mix (page 131)

1 to 3 teaspoons Patak brand mild curry paste, to taste

1 cup frozen green peas

1 cup cooked cubed potatoes

2 tablespoons freshly squeezed lime or lemon juice

In a large pot, mix all ingredients. Cook over very low heat just to heat through, about 5 minutes.

Chili Mix

Makes ³/₄ cup

Authentic chili recipes often include unsweetened chocolate, which gives the dish a savory flavor. Our mix provides a fast way to make a number of different chili dishes.

¹/₄ cup white flour

¹/₂ cup dried minced onion

2 tablespoons chili powder or 1 tablespoon chili powder plus 1 tablespoon Mexican seasoning

2 teaspoons salt

2 teaspoons dried red pepper flakes

2 teaspoons dried minced garlic

2 teaspoons sugar

2 teaspoons ground cumin

2 teaspoons unsweetened cocoa powder

In a jar with a tightly fitting lid, mix all ingredients.

Three-Bean Chili

Makes 6 servings

1 tablespoon olive oil

1 medium onion, chopped

1/4 cup Chili Mix (page 135)

Two (14.5-ounce) cans diced tomatoes

One (15-ounce) can chili beans with sauce

One (15-ounce) can garbanzo beans (chickpeas), drained

One (15-ounce) can black beans, drained

1 teaspoon to 1 tablespoon Mexican seasoning, to taste (optional)

1 avocado, sliced, garnish (optional)

1/2 cup chopped fresh cilantro (optional)

1/3 cup chopped scallions (green onions), including green portion (optional)

In a large pot, heat oil over medium heat, and sauté onion until golden brown, about 5 minutes. Stir in Chili Mix; then add tomatoes, beans, and Mexican seasoning, if desired. Simmer, uncovered, stirring occasionally, over medium-low heat, 10 minutes.

Tofu Chili

Makes 6 servings

1 tablespoon olive oil

1 medium onion, chopped

$^1/_4$ cup Chili Mix (page 135)

2 teaspoons Mexican seasoning

One (14-ounce) package firm tofu, drained and crumbled into bite-sized pieces

One (15-ounce) can Mexican-style stewed tomatoes or diced tomatoes

One (15-ounce) can tomato sauce

1 cup frozen corn kernels

One (15-ounce) can S&W brand Pinquitos or other chili beans with sauce

In a large pot, heat oil over medium heat, and sauté the onion until golden brown, about 5 minutes. Add Chili Mix, Mexican seasoning, and tofu. Stir until tofu is coated with the seasoning; then add tomatoes, tomato sauce, corn, and beans. Simmer, uncovered, stirring occasionally, over medium–low heat, 10 minutes.

Old-Fashioned Meatless Chili with TVP and Beans

Makes 6 servings

⁷/₈ cup boiling water

1 cup dried textured vegetable protein (TVP)

1 tablespoon olive oil

1 medium onion, coarsely chopped

1 clove garlic, minced

¹/₄ cup Chili Mix (page 135)

2 teaspoons Mexican seasoning

One (15-ounce) can diced tomatoes

One (15-ounce) can tomato sauce

One (15-ounce) can chili beans with sauce

6 cups cooked rice

1 cup soy cheese, shredded

In a small bowl, pour water over TVP; set aside until all water is absorbed, about 5 minutes. In a large pot, heat oil over medium heat, and sauté onion until golden brown, about 5 minutes. Stir in garlic, cook until lightly golden, 1 minute (do not brown). Stir in TVP and the remaining ingredients. Simmer, uncovered, stirring occasionally, 20 minutes. Serve over rice and top with soy cheese.

Tabouli Mix

Makes 6 cups

Tabouli is a traditional salad served in many Mid-Eastern households. Its wonderful mixture of flavors, from tangy lemon to refreshing mint, improves when allowed to sit for several hours. As with most grain salads, it is best to serve this dish at room temperature.

6 cups bulgur

$1/2$ cup dried parsley

2 tablespoons salt

2 tablespoons dried mint

1 tablespoon lemon zest (optional)

1 tablespoon dried garlic flakes or granules

$1/4$ teaspoon freshly ground black pepper

In a jar with a tightly fitting lid, mix all ingredients.

Basic Tabouli

Makes 4 servings

Chopped fresh parsley and mint, although not necessary, add a nice touch of extra flavor.

1$^1/_3$ cups Tabouli Mix (page 139)

1$^1/_2$ cups boiling water

$^1/_4$ cup freshly squeezed lemon juice

$^1/_4$ cup olive oil

2 medium tomatoes, chopped

1 bunch (about 6) scallions (green onions), thinly sliced

1 cucumber, chopped (about 2 cups)

Salt to taste (optional)

In a medium bowl, combine Tabouli Mix and water. Let stand until water is absorbed and the bulgur is chewable, about 1 hour. Add remaining ingredients, mix thoroughly, and refrigerate at least 1 hour. Adjust seasonings with lemon juice and salt, if desired, right before serving.

Tips and Variations

If you don't have an hour for the bulgur to soak, bring the water to a boil, add the bulgur, and boil 2 to 3 minutes. Remove from heat, and let sit 15 minutes. Fluff with a fork before adding the remaining ingredients.

Tabouli with Garbanzo Beans and Vegetables

Makes 6 servings

3 cups cooked Basic Tabouli (page 139)

$^1/_4$ cup sliced black olives

$^1/_4$ cup currants (optional)

1 red, orange, or yellow bell pepper, chopped

1 medium carrot, grated

One (15-ounce) can garbanzo beans (chickpeas), drained

Prepare Basic Tabouli. Before refrigerating, stir in the remaining ingredients.

Tips and Variations

Unless you can find good organic cucumbers, use the English or hothouse cucumbers. We no longer consider them an extravagance. Besides being more flavorful, they have a tender skin—not tough and waxy—so they don't need to be peeled, nor do they need to be seeded. Also their tight-fitting cellophane wrapper helps keep them remarkably fresh.

Vegetarian "Meatball" Mix

Makes 3 cups

3 cups all-purpose flour

4 tablespoons salt

2 tablespoons dried minced onion

1 tablespoon dried oregano

1 tablespoon dried minced garlic

1 tablespoon chili powder

$1/4$ teaspoon freshly ground black pepper

Mix together and store in a tightly covered container in a cool, dark place.

Basic Vegetarian "Meatballs"

Makes 6 servings

Try these "meatballs" in your favorite spaghetti sauce.

$7/8$ **cup boiling water**

1 cup textured vegetable protein

1 cup soft bread crumbs

$1/2$ **cup Vegetarian "Meatball" Mix (page 142)**

1 tablespoon soy sauce

Oil for sautéing

In a small bowl, pour the water over textured vegetable protein; set aside. In a medium bowl, combine textured vegetable protein, bread crumbs, Vegetarian "Meatball" Mix, and soy sauce. Mix thoroughly. Form into 1-inch balls. In a large pan heat the oil over medium heat, and sauté "meatballs" in oil until brown.

6

Planovers: Making Yesterday's Leftovers Tonight's New Meal

Our friend Kathy Constantine introduced us to the word *planover* for a wonderful twist on what to do with leftovers. Planovers can take several forms. The most common idea is to double up a recipe so that you have enough for the next evening's meal. Another is to cook up extra quantities of single ingredients. For example, if you are cooking brown rice to serve with chili or beans, make a few extra cups and use it later in the week for rice and lentil salad or curried rice with raisins. A little forethought costs no additional time but makes meal preparation throughout the week easier. Our favorite idea, however, is to allow recipes to evolve into completely new meals. For example, start with our easy Black Bean Soup with Fresh Lime and Cilantro (page 158) and make sure that there will be a couple of cups left over. Then use the soup as a base for making our fast and delicious Black Bean Sauce with rice (page 159) or Black Bean Tostadas with Avocado (page 160). We've provided ten basic recipes on which you can build to keep your meals versatile and interesting but still super easy.

We'll also share some ideas for turning the most basic leftovers into gourmet meals—in a matter of minutes. What do you do when you have a cup of this and a half cup of that in the refrigerator, nothing that really fits into any of your favorite recipes or that seems enough to make a meal? We have some ideas: See "Wraps: Making the Most of

Leftovers" (page 145) and "Gourmet Leftovers" (page 148). And be sure to check our tahini and peanut sauce ideas on pages 108–110, which will quickly turn any leftovers into a delicious meal.

WRAPS: MAKING THE MOST OF LEFTOVERS

Many cultures worldwide use flatbreads, tortillas, chapatis, pancakes, or thin pocket breads as wrappers for foods, creating meals that you can eat with your hands. These wraps have become rather trendy in restaurants all over the United States, and for the home cook, the idea is a wonderful way for stretching leftovers. The easiest wraps to find in supermarkets and co-ops are tortillas, pita bread, and whole wheat Indian chapatis (which are our favorite). They are a great substitute for typical sandwiches, and they travel well for picnics or brown-bag lunches. Some are eaten cold, and others can be popped into a microwave oven for a few minutes.

Even if you are not going to eat your wrap right away, warm the tortilla or chapati first, as this makes it easier to fold and less likely to tear. Place three to four heaping tablespoons of filling (or more if using one of the big tortillas), and fold up the bottom quarter of the bread. Then fold in the two sides before rolling the wrap closed. This makes a neat and portable packet. Or you can leave one of the sides open before you roll up the wrap so that you can add more sauce or salsa before eating.

You can create your own wrap ideas, and they don't require recipes. Here are a few ideas to get you started.

- Leftover Hoppin' José (page 47) mixed with cubes of smoked tofurella cheese or cubed smoked tofu and chopped scallions.

- Black beans and rice with cubes of Monterey-style chili soy cheese and chopped canned jalapeño chiles.

- Red beans, cubed smoked tofu, chopped red bell peppers, and shredded carrots.

- Chili beans, rice, chopped tomatoes, chopped red bell peppers, and onions topped with salsa and sliced avocados.

- Curried vegetables mixed with basmati rice, green peas, and chutney.

- Hummus (page 114), shredded vegetables, chopped cucumber, and chopped tomatoes topped with sprouts.

- Veggie burgers crumbled or cut into smallish pieces with tahini sauce, spinach leaves, and toasted sunflower seeds.

- Baked tofu tossed with Thai peanut sauce or hoison sauce, crispy Chinese noodles, and shredded cabbage.

- Rice and lentils with toasted sunflower seeds and Sesame Shiitake Dressing (page 90).

- Steamed vegetables tossed with basmati rice and topped with Ginger Vinaigrette (page 88).

- Lemony Roasted Potatoes (page 78) mixed with garbanzo beans and Lemon Tahini Sauce (page 108).

- Mock Tuna Spread (page 116) with bean sprouts and shredded jicama.

- Tofu, blanched vegetables, shredded jicama, and Indonesian Peanut Sauce (page 110).

- Diced potatoes, chopped celery, capers, sun-dried tomatoes, egg-less mayonnaise, and Dijon mustard.

- Black beans, chopped green olives, chopped jalapeño chiles, fresh lime juice, and salsa.

- Leftovers from your favorite restaurant. A quarter cup of leftovers may look too small to bother bringing home. But wrapped in a tortilla, it can be tomorrow's lunch.

GOURMET LEFTOVERS

Many times those small amounts of vegetables leftover from a favorite recipe can be combined, with happy results, into a new recipe. For instance, make a pasta salad by adding chopped carrots, broccoli, jicama, and red bell pepper to cooked pasta. Add a can of black-eyed peas, and toss with your favorite salad dressing.

Do the same with leftover grains. Brown rice, quinoa, bulgur, and couscous all make wonderful salads. For every one or two cups of cooked grains, add one can of drained cannellini beans, garbanzo beans, or whatever you like best. Add one cup each of thawed frozen peas and corn, a cup or so of chopped raw vegetables like celery or carrots for some crunch, and about a quarter cup of chopped sun-dried tomatoes. Toss with a vinaigrette, add fresh or dried herbs, if you'd like, and serve at room temperature.

Leftover lentils are perfect in salads with or without the addition of grains. If you have at least two cups of cooked lentils, combine them with two oranges cut into bite-sized pieces, a half cup of currants or raisins, a finely chopped carrot, and a bunch of scallions finely chopped. Toss with Ginger Vinaigrette (page 88), and let sit for several hours. Right before serving add some chopped red and yellow bell peppers and some chopped fresh parsley and mint, if available.

Gourmet vinegars are a nice way to dress up leftovers in just minutes. Toss together leftover rice, quinoa, pasta, or potatoes—whatever you have on hand—and leftover steamed vegetables. Add some balsamic vinegar or tarragon vinegar and a bit of salt and freshly ground black pepper. Toss, and eat at room temperature.

For a taste that is special and unique, perk up your leftovers with seasoned Japanese rice vinegar. It goes with just about anything and adds instant gourmet flavor. Finely shred half a head of cabbage and grate two or three carrots. In a large bowl, toss with a couple tablespoons of flavored rice vinegar (or to taste). And that's it! To soften the cabbage, refrigerate for half an hour if you have time.

Adding a sauce is one of our favorite ways to give leftovers a new life (see recipes on pages 108–111). Any combination of grains, potatoes, pasta, and vegetables can be heated up and topped with tahini or peanut dressing.

If you want to give your leftovers a fresh taste, add chopped fresh herbs like parsley, basil, and cilantro. They will enliven any dish. Fresh herbs will keep for at least a week in the refrigerator. Remove the rubber band or tie that holds the herbs together, remove the lower leaves, wash carefully, and then pop them in a large jar filled with water. Cover the whole thing with a plastic bag and place in the refrigerator. You may need to refresh the water occasionally, but you will be surprised at how long the herbs remain green and tasty.

Southwest Black Beans

Makes 4 servings

Chopped green olives give these black beans a unique flavor. They make a good fast sauce to serve over rice; then, with a few additions, they can be used to create savory enchiladas or chili.

2 tablespoons olive oil

1 large onion chopped

2 stalks celery, chopped

3 cloves garlic, minced

$1/4$ teaspoon cayenne pepper

4 ounces pimiento-stuffed green olives, chopped

Two (15.5-ounce) cans black beans or 4 cups cooked*

One (4-ounce) can chopped chile peppers, mild or hot

Salt to taste

3 cups cooked brown rice or quinoa

In a large saucepan, heat oil over medium heat, and sauté onion, celery, and garlic until tender, 10 minutes. Add the remaining ingredients, and heat through. Serve over brown rice.

If using canned beans, drain only one of the cans; if using homemade cooked beans, include $1/4$ cup of the cooking liquid.

Planover: Black Bean and Corn Enchiladas

Makes 6 servings

2 cups cooked Southwest Black Beans (page 150)

1 cup frozen corn, thawed

One (10-ounce) can mild enchilada sauce

1 cup tomato sauce

Twelve (6-inch) corn tortillas

Chopped scallions (green onions), to taste

Chopped fresh cilantro to taste

Salsa to taste

Preheat oven to 350°F.

In a medium bowl, mix Southwest Black Beans and corn; set aside. In a small bowl, mix together enchilada and tomato sauces. Spread one-half of sauce on the bottom of a baking pan. Spread each tortilla with $1/4$ cup bean mixture; roll, and place seam side down in the baking pan. Pour remaining sauce over the top.

Cover with aluminum foil, and bake 15 minutes. Uncover, and bake until heated through, 5 to 10 minutes. Garnish with chopped scallions and cilantro and serve with salsa.

Tips and Variations

Corn tortillas taste especially wonderful with this dish, but they do tend to disintegrate when you bake them in the sauce. A faster and less messy way to make this dish is to layer the tortillas with the beans instead of rolling them. Spread a casserole dish with sauce, and then cover with a layer of tortillas. Spread half the bean mixture and another layer of tortillas. Top with the rest of the beans and a third layer of tortillas; pour the remaining sauce on top. Bake as for enchiladas.

Planover: Black Bean and Corn Chili

Makes 4 servings

¹/₂ cup boiling water

¹/₂ cup textured vegetable protein

2 cups cooked Southwest Black Beans (page 150)

1 cup frozen corn, defrosted

1 tablespoon Mexican seasoning or 2 teaspoons chili powder

One (15-ounce) can tomato sauce

One (15-ounce) can diced tomatoes

3 cups cooked rice

In a small bowl, pour water over textured vegetable protein; let sit 5 minutes. In a medium saucepan, combine all ingredients; simmer over low heat until hot, about 8 minutes. Serve over rice.

Spicy Lentil Soup

Makes 6 servings

Here is an Indian-flavored lentil soup that offers lots of flavor with little fuss. Garam masala paste is the magic ingredient. Slightly thickened, this soup—with the very tasty addition of dried fruits—can be used as a sauce over rice or can be made into delicate patties.

2 tablespoons extra-virgin olive oil

1 onion, coarsely chopped

2 stalks celery, sliced

2 teaspoons garam masala paste

1¹/₂ cups uncooked lentils

6 cups vegetable broth

Salt and freshly ground black pepper to taste

In a large saucepan, heat oil over medium heat, and sauté onion and celery until tender, 10 minutes. Add garam masala, and stir to coat onions. Add lentils and broth; bring to a boil. Lower heat to a simmer; cook, covered, until the lentils are tender, 45 minutes. Season with salt and pepper, and adjust the spices to taste.

Planover: Spicy Lentils with Dried Fruit over Rice

Makes 4 servings

3 cups cooked Spicy Lentil
Soup (page 153)

3/4 cup chopped dried fruit*

6 cups cooked brown rice

In a large saucepan, combine Spicy
Lentil Soup and fruit; heat thoroughly.
Serve over rice.

Try any combination of prunes, dried apples, apricots, raisins, or other dried fruit, snipped into small pieces.

Planover: Spicy Lentil-Rice Cakes

Makes 4 servings

2 tablespoon extra-virgin olive oil

$1/3$ cup finely chopped onions

1 stalk celery, minced

1 cup cooked Spicy Lentil Soup (page 153)

1 slice of whole wheat bread, crumbled into small pieces

2 cups cooked rice

$1/2$ teaspoon mixed herbs (optional)

Salt and freshly ground black pepper to taste

In a nonstick frying pan, heat 1 tablespoon of the oil over medium heat, and sauté onions and celery until the onions are soft. In a medium mixing bowl, combine onion mixture, Spicy Lentil Soup, bread, rice, herbs (if desired), salt, and pepper. Mix thoroughly. In the same pan you used to cook onions, heat remaining 1 tablespoon of oil over medium heat. Drop lentil-rice mixture by spoonfuls, as you would pancake mix, pressing cakes down slightly (they will be easier to turn if they are not too large). Cook until lightly browned; turn and cook the other side until lightly browned.

Pasta Salad with Sun-Dried Tomatoes and Basil

Makes 4 servings

About any pasta will do, but the rotini mixture of carrot and spinach pasta is especially attractive with the tomatoes and fresh basil. This salad has a lovely flavor; and heated up with broth, it makes a very special and fast traditional Italian soup.

10 to 12 ounces uncooked pasta

^{1}/$_3$ cup oil-cured dried tomatoes, snipped into small pieces

^{1}/$_4$ cup chopped or snipped fresh basil

^{1}/$_4$ to ^{1}/$_2$ teaspoon fennel seeds

1 clove garlic, pressed or chopped or ^{1}/$_2$ teaspoon garlic salt

2 tablespoons oil from oil-cured tomatoes or olive oil

^{1}/$_3$ cup toasted pine nuts

Cook pasta according to package directions until just tender; drain, and transfer to a large salad bowl. Add tomatoes, basil, fennel, and garlic. Add oil; toss to combine. Garnish each helping with toasted pine nuts, and serve hot or at room temperature.

Planover: Pasta Fagioli with Sun-Dried Tomatoes

Makes 4 servings

1 tablespoon olive oil

1 medium onion, coarsely chopped

2 cloves garlic, minced

3 cups vegetable broth

2 cups cooked Pasta Salad with Sun-Dried Tomatoes and Basil (page 156)

One (15-ounce) can small white beans

One (15.5-ounce) can diced tomatoes

Salt and freshly ground black pepper to taste

Italian herbs to taste*

In a large saucepan, heat oil over medium heat, and sauté onion and garlic until onion is tender, 8 minutes. Add the remaining ingredients, and heat thoroughly, about 5 minutes. Season with salt, pepper, and Italian herbs.

*Use your favorite Italian seasonings, such as oregano, basil, and parsley.

Tips and Variations

Snipping herbs or tomatoes with good, sharp kitchen scissors saves time! Your hands may get a bit messy, but there is nothing else—like a cutting board—to clean up.

Black Bean Soup with Fresh Lime and Cilantro

Makes 4 servings

This thick black bean soup is delicious and couldn't be easier. The addition of lime and cilantro give it a special zip. Add more soup mix—and some chile peppers—to make a sauce for grains or a topping for tostadas.

4 cups water

2 cups black bean soup mix

One (15-ounce) can black beans

One (15-ounce) can chili-style stewed tomatoes

1 cup frozen corn kernels

Juice of 1 lime

$1/4$ cup chopped fresh cilantro for garnish

Lime wedges for garnish

In a medium saucepan, add water to soup mix; stir, and bring to a boil. Lower heat, and add beans, tomatoes, and corn. Simmer 3 to 5 minutes. Just before serving, stir in lime juice. Garnish each bowl of soup with cilantro and lime wedges.

Tips and Variations

Look for Fantastic Foods brand Instant Black Bean mix either in a box or in the bulk food section of your grocery store. Or use the contents of two cartons of individual instant black bean soup in a cup.

If you don't have chili-style stewed tomatoes on hand, use regular diced or stewed tomatoes and add $1/2$ teaspoon chili powder.

Planover; Black Bean Sauce

Makes 4 servings

1 tablespoon olive oil

1 medium onion, coarsely chopped

2 cups cooked Black Bean Soup with Fresh Lime and Cilantro (page 158)

$1/4$ cup instant black bean soup mix

One (4-ounce) can mild chile peppers

$1/4$ to $1/2$ cup salsa to taste

4 cups cooked rice (or other grain)

Fresh chopped cilantro

In a medium saucepan, heat oil over medium heat, and sauté onions until tender, 10 minutes. Add Black Bean Soup with Fresh Lime and Cilantro, instant black beans soup mix, and chiles. Cook, stirring occasionally, over low heat, 5 minutes. Add salsa. Serve over rice garnished with cilantro.

Planover: Black Bean Tostadas with Avocado

Makes 4 servings

2¹/₂ cups cooked Black Bean Sauce (page 159)

Eight (8-inch) whole wheat tortillas

1 avocado, sliced

2 cups shredded lettuce

2 medium tomatoes, chopped

1 cup salsa

Prepare the Black Bean Sauce. Place 1 whole wheat tortilla on a plate, and spoon ¹/₂ cup bean sauce on top. Top with avocado, lettuce, and tomato. Serve with salsa.

Mushroom Soup

Makes 4 servings

Mushrooms and miso, both with their own special earthy flavor, go together to create a very tasty and versatile sauce. We love it as a fast soup, and the leftovers are perfect over pasta (with the nice addition of a portobello mushroom) and as a sauce for home-style Shepherd's Pie (page 163).

2 tablespoons olive oil

1 medium onion, finely chopped

1 pound fresh mushrooms

2 tablespoons all-purpose flour

$^1/_4$ cup miso dissolved in 2 cups hot water

2 cups vegetable broth

In a large saucepan, heat oil over medium heat, and sauté onion until tender, 10 minutes. While onion is cooking, wash mushrooms, and chop finely in the bowl of a food processor fitted with the steel blade. Add to onion, and sauté until mushrooms are tender, 8 minutes. Remove from heat, and stir in flour. Slowly add miso mixture, stirring constantly to avoid lumps. Add broth. Return to heat. Bring to simmer over medium heat, and cook, uncovered, 5 to 10 minutes.

Planover: Pasta with Mushroom Sauce

Makes 4 servings

Pass additional toasted pine nuts and sliced scallions at the table.

1 tablespoon olive oil

1 large portobello mushroom, cut into cubes

1 cup cooked Mushroom Soup (page 161)

1 pound cooked angel-hair pasta

1/4 cup toasted pine nuts

Finely sliced scallions (green onions) for garnish

In a large saucepan, heat oil over medium heat, and sauté mushroom until brown, 4 minutes. Meanwhile, in a medium saucepan heat Mushroom Soup over medium heat until heated through, 5 minutes. Place pasta on a platter, and arrange mushroom cubes on top. Pour soup over all. Top with pine nuts and scallions.

Planover: Shepherds Pie

Makes 4 servings

1 tablespoon olive oil

1 medium onion, coarsely chopped

2 carrots, chopped

1 zucchini, thinly sliced

$^1/_2$ cup frozen corn

$^1/_2$ cup frozen green peas or French-cut green beans

1 cup cooked Mushroom Soup (page 161)

2 cups prepared instant mashed potatoes

Preheat oven to 350°F. In a large, deep skillet heat oil over medium heat, and sauté onion and carrots 5 minutes. Add zucchini, and continue to cook until all vegetables are tender. Add corn, peas, and Mushroom Soup. Stir to combine, and cook over low heat until heated through. Pour into a $2^1/_2$-quart casserole, and spread potatoes on top. Bake, uncovered, until piping hot.

Mixed Beans and Vegetables

Makes 4 servings

Use any vegetables or beans you like in this recipe. It's a great way to use up leftovers. And with the addition of textured vegetable protein and Mexican seasoning, it takes on a whole new flavor that is perfect wrapped in tortillas.

1 tablespoon olive oil

1 cup chopped onions

1 cup sliced carrots

1 cup sliced celery

1 clove garlic, minced

One (15.5-ounce) can black beans, drained

One (15.5-ounce) can small white beans, undrained

$^{1}/_{2}$ cup tomato sauce

Salt and freshly ground black pepper to taste

3 cups cooked brown rice

In a large saucepan, heat oil over medium heat, and sauté onions, 5 minutes. Add carrots, celery, and garlic; mix. Cover, and simmer, stirring occasionally, 8 minutes. Add beans, tomato sauce, salt and pepper, and cook 5 minutes. Serve over brown rice.

Planover: Tortillas with Mixed Beans and Vegetables

Makes 4 servings

$^1/_2$ cup boiling water

$^1/_2$ cup textured vegetable protein

1 cup cooked Mixed Beans and Vegetables (page 164)

$^1/_2$ cup tomato sauce

1 tablespoon Mexican seasoning

Eight (8-inch) corn tortillas

1 avocado, sliced

Salsa to taste

In a small bowl, pour water over textured vegetable protein; let sit 5 minutes. In a large saucepan, combine textured vegetable protein, Mixed Beans and Vegetables, tomato sauce, and Mexican seasoning. Cook over medium heat, stirring frequently. Warm flour tortillas in a toaster oven or ungreased frying pan just until soft. Spoon about $^1/_4$ cup bean mixture onto each tortilla. Top with avocado and salsa. Roll tortilla, and serve with additional salsa on the side.

Mexican-Style Baked Beans

Makes 6 servings

This super-easy and tasty recipe is a variation of the Southern-Style Ranch Beans on page 45. We spiced it up with some Mexican flavors. It's delicious as is and also makes a wonderful base for a fast chili.

2 tablespoons canola oil

2 medium onions, coarsely chopped

2 tablespoons prepared mustard

1 tablespoon cider vinegar

Two (15.5-ounce) cans chili beans

One (15.5-ounce) can vegetarian baked beans

One (15.5-ounce) can chili- or Mexican-style stewed tomatoes

In a large saucepan, heat oil over medium heat, and sauté onions until tender, 8 minutes. Stir in the remaining ingredients. Simmer, covered, 20 minutes.

Tips and Variations

If you don't have chili-style tomatoes, use plain stewed tomatoes and add $1/2$ teaspoon chili powder or 1 tablespoon Mexican seasoning.

Planover: Mexican Bean Chili

Makes 4 servings

$^1/_2$ cup boiling water

$^1/_2$ cup textured vegetable protein

2 cups cooked Mexican-Style Baked Beans (page 166)

1 teaspoon chili powder or 1 tablespoon Mexican seasoning

$^1/_2$ teaspoon whole cumin seeds

One (15-ounce) can tomato sauce

4 cups cooked white or brown rice

2 bunches (about 12) scallions (green onions), sliced, including green portion

Chopped cilantro for garnish (optional)

In a small bowl, pour water over textured vegetable protein; let sit 5 minutes. In a large saucepan combine textured vegetable protein, Mexican-Style Baked Beans, chili powder, cumin seeds, and tomato sauce. Simmer over medium heat until tender, 10 minutes. Serve over rice, topped with scallions and cilantro, if desired.

Mediterranean Limas

Makes 4 servings

You can serve these as a sauce over rice. But we love them as a main course served with Lemony Roasted Potatoes (page 98). Then if you want to use left-over Mediterranean Limas to make the Planover soup, you'll have an instant soup with a flavor that is magical.

1 tablespoon olive oil

1 small onion, coarsely chopped

2 cloves garlic, minced

Two (15-ounce) cans limas, undrained, or 3 cups cooked baby limas with $^1/_2$ cup cooking liquid or vegetable broth

One (15-ounce) can diced or stewed tomatoes or 1$^1/_2$ cups chopped fresh

1 teaspoon dried oregano or 1 tablespoon chopped fresh

2 tablespoons freshly squeezed lemon juice

Salt and freshly ground black pepper to taste

In a large saucepan, heat oil over medium heat, and sauté onion and garlic until garlic is lightly browned and onion is tender, 8 minutes. Add limas, tomatoes, and oregano. Simmer 10 minutes. Add lemon juice, salt, and pepper.

Planover: Savory Potato and Baby Lima Soup

Makes 6 servings

2 tablespoons olive oil

$^1/_2$ medium onion, coarsely chopped

3 cups vegetable broth

2 cups diced potatoes*

2 cups cooked Mediterranean Limas (page 168)

$^1/_2$ teaspoon dried oregano

Salt and freshly ground black pepper to taste

In a large saucepan, heat oil over medium heat, and sauté onion until tender, about 8 minutes. Add broth and potatoes. Bring to a simmer, and cook until potatoes are tender, about 15 minutes. Add Mediterranean Limas and oregano, and continue to simmer until heated through, about 5 minutes. Season with salt and pepper.

Or use 2 cups leftover Lemony Roasted Potatoes (page 98) and omit the onion and olive oil. Simply combine the limas, vegetable broth, and potatoes and heat.

Spicy Szechwan Tofu with Peanuts and Ginger

Makes 4 servings

It's the hot red oil (found in the Asian section of most grocery stores) that makes this tofu dish as spicy as you want. Like most other hot sauces, a little goes a long way, so you might want to start out at the low end of the suggested amount. The ginger also gives this dish an added zip. We like it served over rice or ramen or soba noodles, and it is especially good served with Coleslaw Made Easy (page 96).

2 pounds firm tofu, drained

²/₃ cup finely chopped peanuts

¹/₄ cup finely chopped scallions (green onions)

¹/₄ cup soy sauce

4 tablespoons finely shaved gingerroot

2 to 4 teaspoons sugar

2 tablespoons dark roasted sesame oil

2 tablespoons rice vinegar

2 teaspoons toasted sesame seeds (optional)

¹/₂ to 1 teaspoon red chile oil

Wrap tofu in a paper towel, and squeeze out excess water. On a plate, mash tofu with a fork. In a medium bowl, mix the remaining ingredients. Stir in tofu, and let sit so tofu absorbs the flavorings, at least 15 minutes. Serve over rice or noodles.

Tips and Variations

Gingerroot is very fibrous, and we have never had luck grating it as many recipes suggest. Most of the root just seems to end up clogged in the grater. We have found that freezing gingerroot does the trick. You needn't peel the frozen ginger. Rather than cutting it into small pieces, just shave the ends of the root with a large sharp knife. You will get very thin flakes or shavings of ginger that then can be cut into smaller pieces.

Planover: Szechwan Tofu Wrap

Makes 4 servings

If you have a little Szechwan Tofu left, you can make four wraps. The crispy Chinese noodles give them a delightful crunch.

Four (8-inch) flour tortillas

1 cup prepared Spicy Szechwan Tofu with Peanuts and Ginger (page 170)

1 cup cooked rice

1 cup thinly sliced cabbage (or Coleslaw Made Easy; page 96)

$1/2$ cup crispy Chinese noodles

$1/4$ cup chopped pineapple

Place 1 tortilla on each plate. Divide the remaining ingredients on the tortillas in the order listed. Fold in the sides of the tortilla first; then roll up. Serve with lots of paper napkins!

Planover: Spicy Szechwan Soup

Makes 4 servings

Use leftover Spicy Szechwan Tofu with Peanuts and Ginger (page 170) to make a fast soup.

2 cups miso broth (page 70)

1 cup cooked Spicy Szechwan Tofu with Peanuts and Ginger (page 170)

1 cup baby spinach leaves

In a medium saucepan, heat broth over medium heat. Add the remaining ingredients. Simmer 3 minutes.

Creamed Spinach with Sun-Dried Tomatoes

Makes 4 servings

Soft silken tofu can be puréed with any cooked vegetable to create a rich and creamy sauce to toss with pasta, serve over grains, or top a baked potato. Here we've used cooked spinach and added sun-dried tomatoes. The sauce makes a perfect filling for lasagna (our version uses polenta) or can be thinned to make a soup.

2 tablespoons olive oil

1 medium onion, coarsely chopped

One (10-ounce) bag fresh spinach or one (10-ounce) package frozen chopped

$1/2$ cup vegetable broth

$1/4$ cup chopped oil-cured sun-dried tomatoes

1 tablespoon soy sauce

1 teaspoon dried thyme

1 teaspoon garlic-infused olive oil

$1/2$ teaspoon freshly grated nutmeg (optional)

One (12-ounce) package soft, silken tofu

In a large saucepan, heat oil over medium heat, and sauté onion until tender, about 8 minutes. Meanwhile, steam spinach until limp, about 3 minutes. Place onions, spinach, and remaining ingredients in the bowl of a food processor fitted with the steel blade; process until smooth. Return mixture to the saucepan, and simmer over very low heat to heat through, 5 minutes.

Planover: Polenta Lasagna with Creamed Spinach

Makes 4 servings

One (24-ounce) roll of prepared polenta, plain or flavored

Oil for sautéing the polenta

2 cups cooked Creamed Spinach with Sun-Dried Tomatoes (page 173)

8 ounces firm tofu, coarsely crumbled

One (32-ounce) jar spaghetti sauce

Preheat oven to 375°F.

Slice polenta into $^1/_2$-inch slices. In a large, deep skillet heat oil over medium heat, and sauté polenta until lightly browned on both sides, 3 to 4 minutes on a side. In a large bowl, combine Creamed Spinach with Sun-Dried Tomatoes and crumbled tofu; mix.

Remove polenta from the skillet, and set aside. Spread about $^1/_2$ cup spaghetti sauce on the bottom of the skillet. Arrange one-third of the polenta in a single layer on top of the sauce. Spread with one-half of the spinach mixture. Arrange another third of the polenta on top, and spread with the remaining spinach. Top with the remaining polenta. Pour the remaining spaghetti sauce on top. Cover, and cook over low heat until sauce begins to bubble and layers are heated through, about 10 minutes.

Planover: Cream of Spinach Soup

Makes 4 servings

2 medium potatoes, diced

2 cups vegetable broth

1¹/₂ cups cooked Creamed Spinach with Sun-Dried Tomatoes (page 173)

Salt, freshly ground black pepper, and dried thyme to taste

In a large saucepan, combine potatoes and broth, and simmer over medium-high heat until the potatoes are tender, about 15 minutes. Stir in Creamed Spinach with Sun-Dried Tomatoes, and heat gently. Season according to taste. Thin with more vegetable broth if the soup is too thick.

Appendix

Resources for Busy Cooks

Cookbooks for Fast Vegetarian Recipes

Lemlin, Jeanne. *Quick Vegetarian Pleasures.* New York: HarperCollins, 1992.

Lemlin, Jeanne. *Simple Vegetarian Pleasures.* New York: HarperCollins, 1998.

Sass, Lorna J. *Great Vegetarian Cooking under Pressure.* New York: William Morrow, 1994.

Sass, Lorna J. *Lorna Sass' Short-Cut Vegetarian.* New York: Quill, 1997.

Wasserman, Debra. *Conveniently Vegan.* Baltimore: Vegetarian Resource Group, 1997.

Other Good Vegetarian Cookbooks

Grunes, Barbara, and Virginia Van Vynckt. *All-American Vegetarian.* New York: Henry Holt, 1995.

Messina, Virginia, and Kate Schumann. *The No-Cholesterol Barbecue Cookbook.* New York: St. Martin's, 1994.

Schumann, Kate, and Virginia Messina. *The Vegetarian No-Cholesterol Family-Style Cookbook.* New York: St. Martin's, 1995.

Stepaniak, Joanne. *Vegan Vittles.* Summertown, Tenn.: Book Publishing, 1996.

Mangels, Reed. *Simply Vegan,* (Nutrition Section). Baltimore: The Vegetarian Resource Group, 1991.

Melina, Vesanto, Brenda Davis, and Victoria Harris. *Becoming Vegetarian.* Summertown, Tenn.: Book Publishing, 1995.

Messina, Virginia, and Mark Messina. *The Vegetarian Way.* New York: Crown, 1996.

Periodicals for Nutrition Information about Vegetarian Diets

Vegetarian Journal. The Vegetarian Resource Group, P.O. Box 1463, Baltimore, MD 21203. 301–366-VEGE.

Vegetarian Nutrition and Health Letter. Loma Linda University, School of Public Health, 1711 Nichol Hall, Loma Linda, CA 92350. 888-558-8703.

Index